SON OF THE UNDERGROUND

SON
OF THE
UNDERGROUND

THE STORY OF ISAAC LIU,
SON OF "THE HEAVENLY MAN"

Albrecht Kaul

Translated from the German by Helen Birkbeck

MONARCH
BOOKS

Oxford, UK, & Grand Rapids, Michigan, USA

Original German title: Albrecht Kaul, *Sohn des Untergrunds* © Brunnen Verlag
Giessen und Basel 2011, www.brunnen-verlag.de

This English translation © 2012 Lion Hudson.

The right of Albrecht Kaul to be identified as author of this work has been
asserted by him in accordance with the Copyright, Designs and Patents Act 1988.

First published in the UK in 2012 by Monarch Books
(a publishing imprint of Lion Hudson plc)
Wilkinson House, Jordan Hill Road, Oxford OX2 8DR, England
Tel: +44 (0)1865 302750 Fax: +44 (0)1865 302757
Email: monarch@lionhudson.com
www.lionhudson.com

ISBN 978 0 85721 199 6 (print)
ISBN 978 0 85721 260 3 (Kindle)
ISBN 978 0 85721 261 0 (epub)
ISBN 978 0 85721 262 7 (PDF)

Distributed by:
UK: Marston Book Services, PO Box 269, Abingdon, Oxon OX14 4YN
USA: Kregel Publications, PO Box 2607, Grand Rapids, Michigan 49501

Unless otherwise stated, Scripture quotations taken from the *Holy Bible, New
International Version*, copyright © 1973, 1978, 1984 by the International Bible
Society. Used by permission of Zondervan and Hodder & Stoughton Limited.
All rights reserved. The "NIV" and "New International Version" trademarks are
registered in the United States Patent and Trademark Office by International
Bible Society. Use of either trademark requires the permission of International
Bible Society. UK trademark number 1448790.

Quote page 135 taken from the song "Your Grace is Sufficient" by Marty
Nystrom, copyright © 1991 Integrity's Hosanna! Music/Kingswaysongs. Adm.
by worshiptogether.com songs excl. UK, adm. by Kingswaysongs, a division of
David C Cook tym@kingsway.co.uk. Used by permission.

The text paper used in this book has been made from wood
independently certified as having come from sustainable forests.

British Library Cataloguing Data
A catalogue record for this book is available from the British Library.

Printed and bound in Great Britain by Clays Ltd, St Ives plc.

Contents

1

Son of an enemy of the state

From the very beginning, the Chinese state was suspicious of our family. Even as a young man my father had talked about Jesus in many places in China. Countless people had become Christians because of this, and Jesus had changed their lives fundamentally. My father had founded numerous new congregations so that they would keep growing in the faith.

But working as an evangelist was forbidden in China. As I shall explain, preaching was allowed only in the official church, the Three-Self Patriotic Church, which was controlled by the Communist state. Setting up new congregations was illegal. For this reason my father was viewed as an "enemy of the state", and thus his life was often at great risk.

Yet in many areas the people of China had had enough of Communism. They felt empty, and were looking for meaning in their lives. That's why they were so open to faith in Jesus. Whenever my father preached the gospel, things happened.

Life with an "enemy of the state" was dangerous for the whole family. Even before my parents got married, my mum had begun to sense this. She was seventeen and stood with my father in the town hall, waiting to have the marriage registered. He was twenty-one. Their application to marry had been approved, but even so my father was arrested on the spot and driven into town – something apparently needed to be cleared up. He was already well known as an evangelist in the local area, and that alone was enough to brand him a criminal in the eyes of the state police. They didn't want to ban prayer meetings in the villages, but travelling preachers who spread these "mind-numbing superstitions" were too dangerous to the state.

After several months of questioning, beatings, and insults, they let him go again. So my parents' marriage didn't actually take place until almost a year later. But my father didn't stop travelling around secretly and preaching about Jesus. The head of the Public Security Bureau spied on him constantly after his release and arrested him whenever he could find him.

My mother had said yes to marrying my father of her own free will, even though the marriage had originally been arranged by their mothers. She was proud to be marrying a preacher of the gospel, because she too had given her life to God.

When she became pregnant with me, life became very difficult. Her hard work in the fields, poor nutrition during the pregnancy, my father being in prison again, and on top of that the mockery and contempt of the people in our village all made it very hard for her to cope.

For a long time she managed to keep her pregnancy a secret. She suspected that if she didn't, people would treat her as they treated other wives of "enemies of the state" and forced to have an abortion. But from seven months it couldn't be concealed any longer. She couldn't hide herself away either, as other pregnant women did, because she had to go to the fields and take part in village life. So one evening two policemen came round and ordered her to abort the child of an illegal preacher. She was to report to the hospital in the chief town of the district within three days, or else she would be forcibly collected and taken there.

Mum knew what that would mean, having heard the secret reports that were in circulation: a lorry would draw up and the woman would be thrown onto the load area. She would be kept there by means of kicks and blows. Then the lorry would drive over the rough roads with no use of brakes until it reached the town. Most women gave birth to their babies while on this rolling and bouncing instrument of torture. Stillborn – and quite often premature – babies were thrown from the lorry into a grave or hurled over a bridge into a river, and when the mothers finally got to hospital, they were treated like lepers. Many didn't survive this awful torture; some sprang from the lorry to their death. Anyone who hadn't yet lost her baby was subjected to a painful abortion without anaesthetic in the hospital.

In her anxiety my mother took refuge in prayer. Only God could help her now. She had to do without any help my father might have given her, as he didn't even know what a frightful situation she was in because he was unable to have any contact with her from prison. She couldn't "disappear", as all her relatives lived in the same village or else the next one. They would soon find her there. Neither could she go to ground further away, as she didn't know where to go – and, besides, a pregnant woman alone and far from home was always suspicious.

"God, you have given me this child, even though its father is in jail," she prayed. "Preserve this child for me, and it shall live only for you."

On the evening before my mother was due to go to the hospital, I came early into this world. There were no sterilized towels, no instruments, and no medication at hand. A bowl of warm water and a clean hand towel were all that my grandmother was able to lay out in readiness. She was the only help available in this difficult hour.

Happy, even though at the limits of her strength, my mother held me in her arms. Now I was protected by the law and could no longer be killed. God had saved me at almost the last minute.

The fact that I survived those first weeks without an incubator and with no medical assistance was another miracle from God. I am said to have been tiny, wrinkled and pale. Yet, when I see myself in the mirror now – and when I think about how girls look at me – I have to admit that God actually made me quite good-looking!

News of his son's birth was smuggled to my father in prison. He secretly wrote me a letter – my first, though of course I couldn't understand it until much later. In this letter he specified my name – Isaac. The name should signify, he wrote to me: "offered up to God and thus wonderfully used to carry forth the blessing of God". The story of Abraham and his son Isaac always inspired me later on in life. In total obedience to God, Abraham was prepared even to sacrifice his son in accordance with the practices of the people of the surrounding area. But God does not want such cruel sacrifices, and with Isaac he set the scene for the marvellous history of salvation. The implications of my name make me very proud!

Further on in the letter it said: "Isaac, before you were born your father went into prison, even though he had done nothing wrong. All he had done was to spread the gospel. I have only one wish for your life: that you should follow Jesus, as your name says. You shall become a man full of faith and obedience, just like Isaac." At the end he wrote: "My son, we'll see each other in heaven. Your loving Father."

Today I know that at that awful time of torment and anguish he had given up all hope of life. He did not think that he would ever go free. Every day he lived in fear of execution or feared that he wouldn't be able to endure the torture and agony any longer. It seemed clear to him at that time that this would be the first and the last letter he would be able to write to his son.

But one day, when I was four years old, my father arrived home! The political climate had become a little more relaxed, and he was released from prison. My mother could scarcely contain her joy. Incapable of doing any normal work, she ran around the house with a flushed face.

My grandmother travelled into town to discover the precise terms of his release from the Public Security Bureau, but no one took any notice of her and they gave her no information.

But I felt uneasy. What would it be like having a man in our house? Was he perhaps a bad man after all, as the people in the village thought? Because they thought that if someone is in jail, then there's a reason for it. He must surely be a criminal.

And then my father arrived alone, walking into the village that he hadn't seen for four years. Friends had bought him a bus ticket, but he had been released so late in the day that he only just managed to catch the last bus, which stopped ten kilometres from the village. It was bitterly cold. My father could no longer remember how blissfully warm a heated house could be or how it would be to hold his wife to his chest. He longed to take his son in his arms. My father was about to see me for the very first time.

The front door is locked and I have already fallen asleep on my mat. As my mother later told me, Mum and my father greet each other like strangers, and then suddenly like lovers. Eventually my mother wakes me up and says: "Your father has come home."

I hold her hand and move awkwardly to the door to peer distrustfully at this stranger. He crouches down and stretches his arms out to me – but I hide behind my mother. This strange man seems quite sinister to me. What does he have to do with me? Is he bad after all?

Then I see my father go down on his knees. He prays loudly and passionately; he praises God for my life; he extols God's goodness and his will. Then he blesses me.

These tones are familiar to me. While he is praying, I

go to him and fling my arms around his neck. Now we are all kneeling on the stamped-down clay, thanking God for his goodness and his help.

2

A nervous robber

Because my father was constantly on the move and not able to spend much time at home, my grandmother became an important person for me and for the Christian groups in the surrounding villages.

She was a small, self-assured woman. Working in the fields had made her bent, but her feet still faithfully carried her over many kilometres, and she went out most days. I loved her because she made time for me and had filled my heart with the love of God. I went out with her almost every day. Her name was Yun Qing Wu but I called her Nai Nai, which is what paternal grandmothers are called in our area.

She took me with her to secret meetings with other Christians. What with singing, praying, and intensive Bible study, we often wouldn't stop before twilight to return to our village. Then we had to walk through dark, spine-chilling woods, over wide, storm-wracked fields, or along the river with its secretive bends and its eerie gurgling.

I imagined an evil spirit might emerge at any moment from behind that gnarled old tree, from out of those swampy ditches between the rice fields, or from behind a ruined box grave! In the river's mutterings I heard threatening messages. You need to know that our village was characterized by a fear of evil spirits and doom-laden figures. No one would go past the cemetery at night, and even during the day there was always an undefined air of anxiety in the village. The whole of nature was filled with spirits, and not just benevolent ones, or so we believed. So it might well be true that the hollow trees were the dwelling-places of terrible beings that ate up children and cut the hearts out of their living bodies.

The Christians knew full well that this was all just superstition, but the dread of demons and evil gods ran deep in all the inhabitants of our village – and it was nourished by many mysterious incidents and accidents. When I clasped Nai Nai's hand more firmly, she could feel my anxiety. Then she would tell me of God's protection and his faithfulness, that Jesus was bigger than all evil powers, and that we were surrounded by him as if by a protective wall. Her trust in the God of heaven was infectious – until I started once again in fear at the sound of a cracking branch.

On one occasion a robber lay in wait for us on a path through the woods, threatening to stab us to death unless we gave him money. But his voice sounded somewhat nervous, and he brandished his rice sickle rather clumsily.

Nai Nai was much calmer than he was!

"Get out of the way! You won't get anything from us; we are poor people, and anyway we stand under the protection of our Grand Master, Jesus Christ."

The robber seemed frightened. He looked around

anxiously. Maybe he didn't know anything about Jesus Christ, or perhaps the words "Grand Master" reminded him of an expert in Chinese martial arts. At any event, he sprang sideways into the bushes, tripped over a root, and fell flat in the mud.

Though she had successfully chased off the robber, my grandmother ran home more quickly than usual. I could sense her relief as we reached the first houses of the village. For me it was clear from that evening on that the name of Jesus had special power.

3
Our village

Our village was called Liu Lao Zhuang, and it lay in Hubei Province, in Central China. It was a village like thousands of others in that vast central area. There was no industry there, no banks or businesses, no schools, and no doctor. In those days no one had a telephone, a car, or a television.

Around 600 farmers and their families lived in the village. The houses huddled closely together with narrow passages between them, which turned into muddy tracks when it rained. Fields surrounded the village in a haphazard and disorganized manner. The people who had arrived first got the closest areas to cultivate, and the few who moved in later had to go quite a distance to reach their part of the fields.

Most of the residents moved there from the northern province of Shanxi several hundred years ago. There hadn't been enough land available in that region then, and the area around our village was still sparsely populated. Since then, hardly any newcomers had moved in. The people married each other or looked for partners no further away than the neighbouring villages. That was why most people had the name Liu. My grandparents had lived in the village for years. Many of my grandfather's relatives were still at home and were naturally also called Liu.

At the time I was born, on 19 April 1984, there was still a lot of poverty there. Fresh water was available only in the centre of the village, where there was a well from which we had to draw water from a depth of seven metres. We children would often run to the well with a pot and have to wait until an adult or an older child came along to help us. The majority of the residents couldn't read or write, including my grandmother.

The main road between the nearest big towns lay about ten kilometres from the village. By taking rough and bumpy roads we could get to a bus stop on the main road. When it rained, or during the intolerable summer heat, it was an arduous process.

Our house lay near the village square. It was on a slight rise and was therefore easily reachable in all weathers. It consisted of some wooden beams and beaten-down clay. There were no walls inside, but my parents had used hanging mats to make a semblance of rooms. When it rained we were kept busy with repairs. My parents had covered the roof and small courtyard with more or less watertight rush mats, which needed constant mending.

The yard played a big part in our lives. My mother cooked there, I played under the roof, a lot of work was carried out there, and in the oppressively hot summer nights we even slept out there. I didn't have a bed, and nor did my parents. I slept with my sister, Yiling, who was five years younger than me, on mats on the floor. Only my grandmother had a space reserved for her on the *kiang*.

The *kiang* is a sort of structure built over the hearth. This is heated from outside and serves as the kitchen fireplace, the waste heat from it warms the *kiang*. Sometimes, in winter, I was allowed to climb up to share this warm little space with Nai Nai.

We had no electric light either. For illumination we used a paraffin lamp that had been given to my grandfather by a missionary. But it wasn't easy to obtain the paraffin for it. If we tried using different liquids in it, it smoked greasily and little black flecks rained down everywhere. We often sat in the dark in the evenings, or used a single candle to light the whole house.

We sometimes went to the village square to eat our meals. People still met there for lunch. Each person brought a modest portion of food, and the old men and women would tell stories of the past and retell Chinese sagas.

Nai Nai was quite often asked to tell Bible stories. Our villagers liked to hear these, and even the political leaders didn't seem to mind them.

Religion was not totally frowned upon. Many people had a little Buddhist altar in their home. It was often ignored and covered in dust, but when a member of the family got ill or died, relatives would light candles in front of it. In practical terms, belief in gods and spirits played no positive role. There was just that all-pervasive fear of punishment from the gods and of the power of evil spirits.

We didn't have a Buddhist or a Daoist temple in the village. Anyone who took their faith seriously went into town every now and then to make sacrifices in the temple for their ancestors or to give money or burn incense sticks for particular life circumstances. In the temples there was a variety of Buddhas. There were different altars for love, grief, illness, happiness, success at work, and good harvests. If you wanted to safeguard your life in all these areas it meant shelling out a lot of money. Once a year there was a big temple festival with lots of sacrifices and vast amounts of smoke and incense, plus storytellers and travelling entertainers; there were also sweets and music. I once really wanted to go to one of these festivals, but my mum was firmly against it and Nai Nai prayed constantly that I would not be led astray by such desires.

4

My grandmother's equation

I can't remember very much about the evenings in our house. Most of the time I was out and about with Nai Nai in the villages. She was very diligent in evangelism and prayer. She moved around the surrounding villages tirelessly, leading more or less secret prayer meetings. My mother often had to work in the fields till evening, and as I wasn't allowed to stay at home alone, my grandmother would take me with her on her community visits. To start with, she often carried me. She would place her arm round her back and I would sit up there. To this day I don't know how she managed to carry me, often for many kilometres, with her poor bent back.

Many local people got to know me because of this, and I heard some Bible stories hundreds of times. I could soon sing some of the songs from memory. It brought joy to the women to see a five-year-old singing away, knowing the words off by heart. Later, when I was eight or nine, I even gave mini-"sermons", using thoughts of my own. These meetings were part of the "house-church movement". Underground churches are still referred to as such today, in contrast to the "Three-Self Patriotic Church Movement", about which I shall say more later.

Through their prayers I learned something of the worries of these simple people, and of their hopes and their trust in God. But sometimes I fell asleep during the meetings with their long prayers. On one occasion the visitors thought that I was praying ardently, when I had actually fallen asleep on my knees before my chair in an attitude of prayer. We always prayed on our knees – many a mother or tired farmer managed to slip in forty winks while doing so. So they let me pray or sleep. After all, they knew that I had a diligent prayer warrior for a grandmother and an evangelist for a father, so they reckoned that some of it must have rubbed off on me. Occasionally they would forget about me. The dark evenings fell quickly on the village, people would leave to go home, and the room would be locked. When I woke up it would be pitch dark, and I would have to pound with my fists on the door until someone let me out of my prison.

One day, after a long time on the road, we arrived in a village just as the prayer meeting was about to end. The services didn't start at any set time, but took place whenever the people had time after finishing work. It was thus quite common, if others had found their way to the service first, for people to stay only a short while at a meeting and then go away again. So when we met only a few believers after our long walk that day, we had to make the whole exhausting trip all over again. But we were pleased to have met even a few Christians. Sometimes we visited just one family. To my grandmother, each individual Christian was as important as a whole congregation.

Even some of the Christians made fun of my

grandmother, calling her "the lady with the horny knees". Prayer was her great passion. She didn't know what a mathematical equation was, but when it came to prayer she would impress this equation on me time and time again: "Much prayer, much power – little prayer, little power. Prayer equals power."

5
A heroine of the faith

My grandmother had come to faith through the work of the Norwegian missionary Marie Monsen, who had worked with great love and perseverance as an evangelist in her village when my grandmother was a young woman. Marie Monsen had talked over and over to the women and told them that there was a Saviour of all sins. We Chinese knew exactly what sins were because of the many religious persuasions around us. In Daoism and Buddhism we had to make many sacrifices so that we could be free of our sins. Jesus takes our sins away and demands no sacrifice in return, only that we give our life into his hands. At some point Nai Nai accepted Jesus into her life. By the time all foreign missionaries were forced to leave the country in 1950, she was already a Christian.

Her faith had grown in the face of many difficulties. In the 1950s the Communists imposed the collectivization of agriculture. All the men and women of the village worked together in the fields, which now belonged to the state. Private ownership had been abolished.

There were of course different attitudes to work. Many people were hard-working, but there were also many who just stood around chatting, urging the others to get on with the work. Worst of all were the agitators. They kept on and on at the farmers, pushing them to ever higher achievements, while doing nothing themselves. But they would shoot their mouths off in the meetings, and anyone who argued against them was branded a counter-revolutionary. He or she would then be set on a path of humiliation and disadvantage.

The harvest would be brought in to the village's communal store. Every day the people would go there to fetch enough rice, flour, maize, and vegetables for their family. If there were ten people in a family, they got ten portions. My grandmother's family consisted at the time of six people, so they were allocated six portions. But because distribution was in the hands of the Communist officials, it was often difficult for my grandmother, especially when there weren't enough provisions to go round.

"We have heard that you are a Christian. So whom do you actually believe in, then?" she was asked by one of those responsible for distribution.

"I believe in the God of heaven and earth, who made us and has saved us through Jesus," replied my grandmother, with no trace of suspicion.

"Right, in that case this God can provide you with food. Put a bowl out in your yard, and tomorrow it'll be full of rice – if your God wants to feed you."

For several days she didn't get as much as a grain of rice for the six people in her family. She was humiliated again and again and even chased with blows out of the depot. In the end they made her wear a "heretic hat" – a pointed red cardboard hat, with big letters proclaiming that she was an anti-Communist and an enemy of the state. The villagers pelted her with rotten fruit and mud. They had to do this because anyone who didn't take part could quickly be branded a counter-revolutionary themselves.

My grandmother couldn't bear this humiliation. In the end she denied her faith and stated that she no longer believed in Jesus but in the victory of the great proletarian revolution. She publicly renounced Jesus and was finally able to obtain the desperately needed provisions.

The following days were dreadful for her. She suddenly heard the words of Jesus: "Whoever disowns me before men, I will disown him before my Father in heaven." She had become a traitor, a Judas.

Nai Nai ran to the woods that night and was about to hang herself. As she looked around with tear-blurred eyes for a tree to which she could fasten her rope, she heard amid her own sighs a warm, melodious voice: "Jesus loves you. Nothing can separate you from his love. He is sticking by you; trust him."

Then she cried for hours for shame and for joy. She tied the rope around a tree, and afterwards she would often go into the wood and pray at this tree, thanking God for the grace of his forgiveness.

The pressure from the Communists grew heavier and heavier, however, until she no longer openly professed her faith in Jesus. She did all she could to avoid having to make a stand, but she never praised Communism again either. For many years she lived out her faith in secret. She kept quiet. She was too afraid of denying her Lord again.

The Communists had achieved their aim where she was concerned.

Only after the Cultural Revolution (between 1966 and 1976) did she regain her courage, because the Communists couldn't do anything about the many prayer meetings in people's houses. My grandmother soon became the point of connection between the rapidly arising groups, and diligently visited all the prayer meetings. She didn't have a Bible, because she couldn't read. But God had equipped her with an amazing memory. She knew many stories from the Bible word for word, and could recite psalms too without error. I think she actually knew all the psalms off by heart – and she often used them as prayers.

Only a few Christians had a Bible in those days. Scraps of paper with Bible texts scribbled on them were very popular. They were more practical, too, for when the police stormed a prayer meeting looking for Bibles and other literature, one could quickly make a slip of paper disappear – by eating it if necessary.

My grandmother's faith in God was an immense encouragement in my life. One day we got home late from an evening meeting. I went out into the garden with her again; she wanted to look over to the right – perhaps she suspected something. We peered into the persimmon tree in which our forty chickens always perched to sleep. But all the chickens were gone. There was no trace of a battle with a fox or any other animal – they had been stolen!

This was a great loss to us. No eggs to eat and swap, no meat on holidays, no giblet broth, and no salted chicken feet, which were a particular delicacy.

I began to cry, but my grandmother comforted me by saying that God himself would take care of us. I never knew how, but when Nai Nai said it, then it was so.

And so it was this time, too. The other Christians of the community not only commiserated with us over our loss, but also brought eggs with them, and many gave up a hen from their own flock, so that our yard slowly filled up again.

I have to say that this was quite unusual for Chinese people. The other families in our community were also poor, and none of them could really spare a hen or even an egg. Normally the Chinese are concerned chiefly with the family, and help is given almost exclusively within the family. When someone was robbed, as we were, then that was just bad luck or fate. The others were merely happy that it hadn't happened to them. But help other people? No, their own family were responsible for that. But here was evidence that the Christian community was a new family. Quite often it was the case that we wouldn't have survived without their help.

6

I only knew my father from the wanted poster

In our village of Liu Lao Zhuang there was, of course, a congregation that had been founded by my father. He had become a Christian after my grandfather had experienced a miraculous healing, and had begun to evangelize at the age of just seventeen. He spoke of God's greatness and reported what God had done for my grandfather. You couldn't call it preaching, because my father was at that time still a very bad speaker. He had "too short a tongue", as the Chinese say, and his pronunciation was unclear. Nevertheless, many in the locality were converted, and congregations were established in the villages around ours.

In our village they used to meet at our house. Our little apartment was soon too small, and people had to stand in the yard and in the street outside the open front door. The Communist rulers of course did not like this, and so my father was imprisoned for the first time at the age of twenty-one.

My grandmother continued the prayer meetings, but the Communists left her in peace. The farmers were ordered not to believe in this foreign "imperialist cult", but many would not be kept away from the places of prayer. In their hearts they had become new people, and they allied themselves to Jesus.

In the villages we were actually able to gather together quite freely. The Party leadership didn't really want to take strong action. In fact, more and more state employees joined the community. Police raids were now centred on the main towns. They came out to us only to check whether we had any foreigners visiting our community – or because they were looking for my father again, who for them was always an enemy of the state. When he had been active only in our community, they would let him be. But for him to travel around founding so many new congregations was definitely a crime in the eyes of the authorities.

As I have already recounted, I didn't get to know my father until I was four years old. I knew of course that he was the famous "Brother Yun", for whom many people prayed. I knew that he was in prison and condemned to a long sentence because he had been a successful evangelist and had set up countless congregations. But what a father was? Of that I had no idea. I knew from some children that their fathers beat them. Others proudly told of all the great things their fathers could do.

For quite some time my father appeared on a wanted poster. So I did at least know what he looked like, but apart from that I could get no real impression of him. I really knew only my mum, Nai Nai, and a few female neighbours. The men in our village scarcely paid me any attention, and only a few came to our prayer meetings.

None of them bothered with me. Only toothless old Shei waved me over every now and then and handed me a corn on the cob or a few cherries. He also taught me how to bore a hole in a plank or a stick using a knife, whereupon I felt very proud of myself and bored several holes in our furniture – much to my mother's dismay.

7

My mother was a very courageous woman

My mum had little time for me because she was the only one who could work in the fields. We had been given five shares of the village's field area by the Party, one for each member of the family. My grandfather was now dead and my grandmother far too old for agricultural labour. My father languished in prison and I was still just a little child. So my mother had to manage this fairly large area of land on her own in order to bring in our quota of the harvest. Then she had to deliver it to the village elders. She only rarely had any help from the men and women of the community, because she was supposed to bring in her quota by herself.

Sometimes the Hoa brothers came to help us. The older brother was very strong and really got down to it. Some days they did as much work as my mother could do in a week.

The younger brother, Hoa Qin, would often play with me too. Those were happy times for me, because he was so funny. I was allowed to ride on him as on a horse. He carried me on his shoulders to our house in the village and we would do tai chi like the grand masters, although our version had little in common with this traditional martial art. Even today he will still relate, to everyone's amusement, how I once did a pee on his head because I was laughing so much.

But such carefree times were few and far between. My mother cried a lot in those years. Many people in the village could not understand why her husband was in prison. If he were a decent farmer he shouldn't be behind bars, in their opinion. Other Christians hadn't been incarcerated, so he must have done something bad.

In addition to this, my mum didn't really have a clue about farming. In her parents' house her tasks had been cooking and housework. Her five siblings had worked on the land at that time. Now she of all people had to cultivate such a large acreage.

But God stood at her side in this as well. It was important for us to bring in a good yield so that we could deliver it to the village leaders. If we did so, our share of the allocation from the central provisions store would be assured for the whole of the year. We had no other income from rearing animals or factory work.

As an example, my mum planted sweet potatoes. But she stuck them in so far apart that the other farmers laughed at her. Even the children made fun of my mother, which was hard for her to bear. But at the end of the summer came the harvest, and my mother dug bigger sweet potatoes out of the ground than anyone in the village had ever seen!

She also didn't know how to sow wheat. She scattered the seeds much too closely together, and became a laughing stock again. But when a hailstorm destroyed all the crops in the area, our fields weren't as badly damaged because the wheat was so dense. These things were hints of the love of God for us – and that he was carrying us through this time, even if we had to do without my father.

At that time God also provided us with a bridge to reach other people. It was a very dry summer, and the wells in the yards and in the village square stopped giving water. Then we discovered a well in our own yard, which my grandfather had dug years ago. This still had water, so now the people came to us and asked for water. My mother was very trusting and let them scoop up the water themselves. She was of course concerned that our well might dry up too, but she trusted that God would keep filling it up, just as he had done with the widow of Zarephath's jug of oil in the Bible.

Sometimes the people would be standing waiting with their pots and buckets as early as five in the morning, so there was lots of opportunity to talk. Many were surprised by my mum and grandmother's open generosity. Such behaviour is very rare in China, as I've already said. Material assistance is normally only directed towards family members and other relations, not strangers – and certainly not those who say bad things about you. So our family's standing improved in the eyes of the village. Many new visitors came to the prayer meetings as a result of all this, and became Christians. Generosity stemming from faith in God was the best possible sermon, understood by all.

8

Persecuted, but alive and active

The political situation changed in 1988. A law was passed bringing in general freedom of religion in China. The official church, the Three-Self Patriotic Movement ("self-determination", "self-support", "self-propagation"), was promoted by the state. No money was paid, but the authorities urged the Christians to join it. That way they could live out their faith unhindered in China.

These official churches with their freely accessible services were easier for the authorities to control. But those who didn't submit to the dictates of the state set themselves up in opposition to the law. Many of the house churches did not trust the state and didn't link up with the Three-Self Church. My father was one of those asked to cooperate with the representatives of the Three-Self Church, but he would have none of it. Being that close to the state was so repugnant to him that it was a step he just couldn't take.

Following the massacre at the "Gate of Heavenly Peace" in Beijing on 4 June 1989 (also known as the Tiananmen Massacre), the government decided in May 1991 to take a harder line with the many house churches that had sprung up all over the country. Although a law had been passed to dissolve the house churches, they had been growing even more, thanks to the work of travelling preachers, and through the direct intervention of miracles from God. The leaders of the house churches were trying to make contact with overseas Christians, an action that was punishable as counter-revolutionary by the Communist government. Yet the movement could no longer be checked by the state, not even by means of arrests and cruel persecution.

So we carried on meeting in our village for prayer and church services. The greater the pressure became, the more people accepted the gospel. Even some Communist leaders joined our community and made no secret of the fact that they had found a new and joyful way of life.

In our village we had a fairly good relationship with the political leaders. They knew that we Christians were not about to overturn the state, and they also noticed that we worked hard, looked after the underprivileged, and were developing a sense of concern for the protection of the environment as well. The common view in Party circles was that nothing better could happen to the Chinese state than for many to become Christians and lead a responsible life. But of course no one could admit this, because it would have called into question the fundamentals of the Communist ethos.

During this time, my father was let out of prison subject to certain conditions, such as that he must always report to the local police when he wanted to leave the village. At the beginning he did indeed do this, but eventually he started going off travelling again for days without reporting and asking for permission. Until they arrested him again.

One of the things he set up secretly with some friends was proper training for the leaders of local house churches. He was indefatigable in his travels. He spared neither himself nor his family, and allowed himself no rest. So in the end it was God himself who put the brakes on, as my father said to me, and he was sent to the notorious labour camp at Da'an. My father had been accused of "unauthorized assembly" and planning an "uprising", because he had been meeting foreigners.

It wasn't clear to me at the time how my father managed to harmonize this imprisonment with God's will. Over and over again I asked myself: why would God let this happen?

9

It's a good thing you only get baptized once!

We would often have Holy Communion as part of our prayer services – much more often than in evangelical and free churches in Europe. This was a real high point of our community life. There was lots of singing, and confession played a large part in it. Everyone acknowledged his or her sins before God and also before the people. Both men and women went up to one another and asked for forgiveness for unChristian conduct and bad thoughts. When two people admitted their guilt to each other they would often cry, first with remorse and then with joy. People who had previously only spoken harshly of each other now held each other in their arms. There was a sense of genuine repentance and great joy at such forgiveness. The new relationships were so honest and so heartfelt that I just wanted to be part of it all.

Praising God the Father and thanking him for the death of his Son and for his victory over sin took up much of the time. At Communion each person received the bread and wine, though we often only had water for the latter, over which the minister would utter a fervent prayer.

But I wasn't allowed to take part because I was not yet baptized. As an eight-year-old boy I had a great longing to join in and receive Holy Communion too. So it was my sincere wish to be baptized as soon as possible.

One night the whole community set out in the dark to walk three miles past the next village to the river. We had to be careful, of course, so we went in small groups. We were told to keep silent when we passed a village. Normally, whenever we went to prayer meetings in other areas, we would encourage the inhabitants of the villages through which we passed to come with us. And we liked to sing aloud as we went, because our gospel songs conveyed many biblical messages.

But at this particular baptism service we wanted to be by ourselves. We didn't want the security forces to get suspicious of us. We might not all have been arrested, but we didn't want to be disturbed anyway.

It must have been in November or December, as I can still recall that it was horribly cold. My mother and my grandmother were there, my grandmother carrying a thick blanket. Around thirty other members of the congregation were baptized along with me, among them the head of the regional government finance department. A lot was at stake for him, but he wanted to belong properly to the congregation.

We sang two songs – singing by heart, naturally, but not as loudly as we Chinese usually like to sing. Then the baptismal gospel was read, followed by a short sermon of only thirty minutes. After that came a lot of prayer and praise that God was so powerful. We thanked him that heaven stood open to all the sinners who were being saved that day.

A lay pastor got into the water and asked us to come to him one by one. I was the first and walked with timid steps into the bitingly cold water. I wasn't as tall as the other candidates, so I stood almost up to my neck in the river. Although my very soul was now freezing, I had to answer three questions:

"Why do you want to be baptized?"

"Because I want to belong completely to Jesus."

"Who is Jesus to you?"

"He is my Lord, who has saved me from my sins and given me new life."

"What does it say in these Bible passages: John 3:16; Matthew 28:18–20; Psalm 23?"

With my teeth chattering but without pausing I was able to reply: "For God so loved the world that he gave his one and only Son, that whoever believes in him shall not perish but have eternal life." And: "Jesus says: 'All authority in heaven and on earth has been given to me. Therefore, go and make disciples of all nations, baptizing them in the name of the Father, and of the Son and of the Holy Spirit, and teaching them to obey everything I have commanded you. And surely I am with you always, to the very end of the age.'"

When it came to Psalm 23 the congregation joined in with me, delighted by my fluent answers. If the pastor hadn't been satisfied with my replies I would have had to wait another year for my baptism. I'm sure the prospect of having to enter that ice-cold water once again gave my soul wings, so that I was able to satisfy him completely with my responses.

Then I was dipped beneath the water three times, and blessed. I was thinking: "It isn't so bad. If I die of cold now, I'll go straight to heaven." My knees shook so much that I could barely climb back up the bank, but my heart was rejoicing: I was now a real Christian. My Lord and Master was Jesus Christ. My home was in heaven.

For the moment, however, I was just grateful that my grandmother was standing on the bank waiting to wrap me in the blanket. At that very point I made up my mind that I would happily become an evangelist, but not a baptizer – he still had twenty-nine more candidates to help into heaven!

10
Not a little saint

I n our village school I had friends who spoke a lot of nonsense to me. But one day when my father was once again arrested, even the teacher couldn't restrain herself from humiliating me in front of the class.

"Isaac and his family are very stupid; they believe in the Christian God. Isaac's father is a criminal, who is serving a well-deserved sentence in prison. He is an enemy of the state and has spread un-Chinese teachings, which have already done a lot of harm to our people."

Not until later did I discover the background to this hatred of Christians. One of the reasons for being against them was of course that Communism rejected all belief in God. But it was also because Christianity had come to China with the brutal opium traders and European conquerors. The missionaries had come with sincere intentions and real love for the people, but they had used methods that the military and economic powers of Europe had established. So at the time it was considered that Christianity had robbed the Chinese of their history and culture. People would say: "One more Christian means one less Chinese." This hatred had made life very difficult for the first missionaries and it had continued down to the

Communist period; in fact traces of it remain to this day.

So the children soon took up the teacher's motto. They even beat me up and accused me of being an enemy of the state. I said nothing of this to my mother, because she already had enough to worry about and was so concerned about my father, from whom we had heard nothing for a long time.

But when one day I announced that I didn't want to go to school any more, she wouldn't let me be until I had given her the real reason. She cried a lot and held me for a long time. She was also worried by the thought that this persecution still awaited my sister, Yiling. I had the impression that she was suffering more than I was. For this reason I summoned up my courage and returned defiantly to school.

When I was about nine I began to read the Bible myself. My father had received this Bible from an old preacher, who had wrapped it in oiled paper during the Cultural Revolution and buried it. It was a real treasure to my father and our family, but I found it very hard to read. In school we learned the new Chinese language with the simplified letter symbols, but this Bible had been written in the traditional characters. Luckily I had heard almost all the stories already, and knew many by heart.

We Chinese set great store by learning the Bible off by heart. In times of persecution, no one can take this knowledge away from you. My father went to a lot of trouble to make sure that I learned much of it in this way. When he came back from his evangelism trips or when he had been working in the fields during the day, I would always have to recite a chapter from the Bible. I had to slave away at the well-known verses, and now I was even getting homework. And if I was unable to recite the set verses, I would have to fast – which is what my father called it when, as punishment, I had to go without supper.

That was a harsh punishment for a growing boy. We didn't have enough to eat to start with, and now this hardship on top! I began to hate the Bible, and no longer read it with enthusiasm.

I didn't love my father very much either at that time. He was simply away too often. When he wasn't in custody he was off on evangelism tours, and when he finally did come home I was questioned on my prepared chapters.

Today I know of course that this drastic form of Bible study did me good. My father has become a great and a good friend to me, and I'm grateful to him for my life and for everything that I have learned from the Bible. I often wonder at how little Western Christians actually know of Holy Scripture. How can the word form us and guide us if we don't know it? So, yes, I *am* grateful to my father for making me cram the Scriptures.

In summer we had three months of holiday. That was the happiest time in the life of the village. When we were children we would set out to discover nature – sometimes we destroyed it as well, I am sorry to say, but we didn't understand this at the time. When the sweet potatoes had been harvested, our parents sent us out into the fields to dig around. In this way we brought home treasures that the farmers had missed. Sometimes it amounted to half a sack of potatoes.

But we also provided ourselves with other food, something I'm a bit ashamed of now: we made catapults out of forked branches and rubber bands, and shot at birds. The smaller birds were merely target practice; they died for no good reason. But the bigger ones were carried happily and proudly home, as they would enhance the family menu.

Sometimes we would fasten iron spikes to bamboo sticks and go hunting frogs. Even these were a welcome change to our family's diet. My grandmother was particularly skilled at making a decent stew out of frogs' legs and a tasty soup out of the rest of the frog. Once when we captured a big tortoise the whole family had a real feast.

When we went fishing, we village children used a specific technique. We stretched some foil over a bowl and cut a hole in the foil. We placed a few bits of bread in the bowl and submerged it in the river. Fish came during the night to nibble at the bread. To do this they had to swim through the hole in the foil, but they weren't able to get out again. In the morning we would run down to the river and gather in our harvest. But sometimes the entire bowl was missing; either the current had carried it away or other children had stolen our fish trap. My mother was always annoyed when we lost yet another bowl, because they cost money and you had to go into town to get a new one.

No way could you have called me a little saint. Naturally, I devised pranks and could be cheeky. The catapult was part of our standard equipment as boys. We carried our catapults all the time – including in school. You just never knew when something might pop up on the way to school that you could kill. I even played around with it in the schoolyard, and on one occasion "killed" a windowpane. As I was a pastor's child, this might have been viewed as retaliation against the state-run school. My father had just been imprisoned again, so a new pastor had to come to sort it out with the school and the Party leadership. And the pane had to be replaced as well, of course, but I was relieved that there were no worse consequences.

The other boys had taught me how to whistle with my fingers in my mouth. I used this new skill with enthusiasm, and let loose a daring whistle one day during class. Everybody laughed, and the teacher wanted to know who had whistled. But I was too cowardly to admit it and the others did not give me away. They were proud of their success at teaching me.

So we boys were all frogmarched out of the classroom and caned on our backside outside the door. I was pleased that the other boys put up with this with good humour and didn't pay me back for the caning. That would have meant thirty-three more blows – the number of boys in the class with me.

Another time I was playing with matches at school. A match would be placed with its tip on a rough surface. The thumb of the left hand held it in place, and then you flicked the match away with a finger. If it was done properly, the match would fly off, bursting into fire as it flew.

On one occasion I managed to do it very well, but there was a problem with my aim. One of my burning matches flew straight at the neck of one of the girls, set her hair alight and left her with a nasty burn. She has probably still got the scar. My guilty conscience pricked me severely for that. I was worried that people would now speak badly of us Christians: "Yes, those Christians set fire to girls and mutilate them. One day that pastor's children will set fire to the whole village. It's quite right that the father should already be in prison."

Thoughts like this ran through my head. But luckily the girl's family were among the faithful in the village, and I made my tearful apologies to them. I would also often give the girl little presents after this: a pen, a juicy orange, or a stick of candy, which I would really rather have eaten myself. She accepted everything without a word, or even so much as looking at me, and never said thank you. I must have hurt her feelings badly, quite apart from the burn itself. Whenever I think of that stupid prank now, I wish I could meet the young lady again and be reconciled with her.

11

Police and demons

Our church community continued to meet in our house or in other private homes. We had no community room of our own. When it wasn't safe to meet in the village, we would gather in the woods or in a sort of bay on the riverbank, which wasn't easy to spot. It was amazing how the information got around about the meeting: the whole congregation was always there, even in the most secret of places.

When the authorities started persecuting us more strictly again, we met now and again in the cemetery. Many of the new Christians found that a bit creepy, but the brothers and sisters in charge encouraged us and said: "The devil's demons and the evil spirits of the ancestors have no power any more – Jesus is the victor and he has risen from the dead. If a spirit should meet us while we're in the cemetery, it can only be one of the resurrected ones…"

It was early in the year. My father was once again on the run. Our house was under constant surveillance because the police wanted to seize my father at all costs. They were hoping that he would return home in disguise or at night. It clearly wasn't possible for the congregation to gather at our house, so we arranged to meet in the cemetery. But the police got word of this and planned to arrest us all.

Five policemen were sent from the main district town to our village. When they heard that we were in the graveyard, they wouldn't go in. The officer in charge grew angry and wanted to force the other policemen to enter the cemetery and take us all into custody. But they were so afraid of the spirits that they wouldn't set foot in the place. They stood several metres away, and moved not a step closer. Their leader raged so loudly that we could all hear him from inside the cemetery.

Eventually the policemen got into such an argument that they turned on each other and started fighting. We could hear the noise from the graveyard and brought the service to a premature end. We slipped silently out of different parts of the cemetery into the night. Some of us, however, went over to the police to care for them, devising makeshift bandages for the injured ones.

But every now and then we did have to deal with real demons and evil spirits, like those in the Bible. In our locality there were some people suffering from possession. They were people who had got locked into a fearful dependency because of superstition or occult practices. Many lived in the woods or in caves by the river. Strange objects were festooned around these caves and in their bamboo huts. Dolls made of rice straw and bark hung from the trees. We didn't really know what these possessed people got up to in secret. But sometimes people from the village would go out to them and take sick children or animals with them, so that they might be healed by magic spells.

These magicians and sorcerers had an oppressive effect on me. They seldom came into the village, and I don't actually know what they lived on. We children were always afraid of these people, because when we did see them, they looked wild and unkempt. When they looked at us, it felt as if they were spearing us with their eyes.

Every once in a while one of these sorcerers or ghost-women would visit our prayer meeting, agitating the believers. But my grandmother would just walk bravely up to them and call out the name of Jesus over and over, for she was certain that these people were possessed by demons. Sometimes they would cry out when she did this and even become violent. On one occasion ten men of the congregation couldn't restrain one of the women, who struck out like a wild thing and actually bit some of the men so badly that they bled. We children were usually taken out of the room at this point, but we could still hear the shouting and the horrible curses of the demons.

One day I was present at the driving out of a demon. We had just begun the prayer meeting and were singing some of our favourite gospel songs when a man suddenly entered the yard cursing, his eyes angry and piercing. It was summertime and we could gather freely in the open. As the man began to hit the faithful with a stick and knock some of the song books out of their hands, my grandmother approached him with great courage and said: "You evil demon, I command you to hang yourself."

At that very moment the man rose from the floor and floated half a metre above the flagstones. He made all sorts of gesticulations but couldn't move from the spot, and didn't hit anyone else with his stick.

He kept on abusing and cursing, but the congregation now began to pray out loud for him, very loudly in fact. Some commanded the evil spirit; others praised God for his redeeming power and for the fact that Jesus was stronger than all demons.

The man's movements grew steadily weaker and it was clear that his peculiar suspended position was taking most of his strength.

Then Nai Nai asked: "You evil spirit in this man, will you come out now and leave this man in peace?"

The man suddenly got his strength back and yelled and writhed.

At this my grandmother called out: "You demon from Satan, I command you to turn upside down." As we all watched, the man revolved so that his head now hung down near the floor – still floating in the air. His movements now became quite ponderous, his cursing ceased, and all he could do was to wheeze out a few bad words.

The congregation, who had by now all gathered around the man, prayed again. Shaken by the man hanging in the air and by the reality of the demons, they praised God loudly and kept on calling out the name of Jesus over the man. The tiny yard echoed with the calls of Jesus; I should think the whole village must have heard them. It must have gone on for about two hours. Darkness had fallen by this time, and I was very frightened by the man hanging in the air.

Finally my grandmother asked again whether the evil spirit would now like to come out of the man. At this the man let out such a terrible cry that we all shrank back in fear, and then he fell to the ground as if dead.

Nai Nai went up to him, shook him gently and asked whether he would accept Jesus into his life. He was free now and would need a new master, or the demon would come back.

The man wept and could only stammer that he would gladly have Jesus in his life. He didn't want to be tormented by such a dreadful spirit ever again.

My grandmother spoke a long prayer of deliverance over him, and he repeated every word haltingly, but clearly deeply moved. Now the whole gathering praised Jesus and his power, and at last the visitors made their way home, visibly shaken.

I have known ever since then that demons are real, but I have also experienced the greater and stronger power of Jesus.

Nai Nai could have recounted other similar experiences, but she didn't like to, because she didn't want to acknowledge and draw attention to the power of demons.

One day the police came to our house yet again. The policemen were looking for my father. They searched the whole house and spotted the many certificates that I had been awarded for achievements at school and in sport.

These were all hanging neatly in line and filled almost one entire wall of our central room.

One of the policemen examined them very closely and then said: "I can see that you are going to do great things for China."

"Indeed," agreed Nai Nai. "He's going to be a preacher of the gospel."

Nonplussed, and minus my father, the policemen drove away again.

12
Secret meetings

We had discovered a good system for passing on information. It had come about because of our group responsibilities. We were divided into groups of five, fifty and one hundred, with one person responsible for each group. Because of my wide knowledge of the Bible I had become the leader of a group of five when I was just ten years old. Being allowed to lead this group made me feel very honoured and important. I kept inviting other youngsters to join, because I had staked my honour on expanding our group so fast that a new group of five would soon have to be formed from it. I wanted to be just like my father, who had set up many congregations.

This was a very positive experience for me, because I didn't get any other kind of recognition from the village. In school I was an outsider. They called me "little Jesus". That could of course have been a mark of respect, but in fact was meant in a mocking and contemptuous way. I was also despised because my father was so often in prison. My mother was also sharply criticized because she had children and apparently no husband. The minds of the village people were always rather simple and easily influenced by Communist propaganda.

So that we would still have a safe place to meet even when the police decided to disturb the services held in our homes, the church community built a few extra hidden assembly points. I still remember how my father once took me with him to Nanyang, where the congregation had dug out a sort of cave as a meeting place. We went into a house built into the side of a mountain. The house didn't look anything special; there were hundreds like it in that area. But the garden had only recently been laid out. The soil was newly turned and in it were flowers, bushes, and new vegetable patches.

The stones that had been dug up during this work had been taken away at night and used to build a new little "building" with one room, in which my father had lived in secret for two years. Behind a stack of firewood in the kitchen of the main house lay the concealed entrance to this cave. When you pushed the pile of wood aside you could see a dark hole in the wall. On one visit we crawled with a candle into this hole, which turned into a passageway about one metre high. Bent double, we took a few steps into the mountainside and then the passage opened out into a space big enough to hold sixty to seventy people.

It contained simple benches and two oil lamps on the wall. Sixteen people were gathered there; they turned out to be running a secret Bible school. My father and some other brothers in the faith were training future house-church leaders in this very room.

Among the books on a shelf on the wall were some interesting-looking foreign ones, which were strictly forbidden. But I was more interested in reading theological books in the Chinese language. I would gladly have taken some home with me, but it was too risky.

After two hours, most of the air in the cave had been used up, and I began to feel quite ill. One of the older ladies fainted, so we all had to go out to get some air. They really should have bored an air shaft, but the local church community lacked the necessary tools and, anyway, who would do the work? Every now and again a brother who had managed to get hold of some larger tools would carry out some work for the secret house churches, but it was always dangerous.

One of the brothers worked in a steelworks at the time. When his congregation decided to build an extension to their church, he acquired a steel girder from the works. Of course this wasn't really very ethical, but it was quite normal for the workers to help themselves to a bit of steel when they had need of it. One of them had even taken enough girders to build a seven-metre-long bridge so that he could get from his house to his fields on the other side of the river. When this came out he was publicly scolded and forced to collect the exact same weight in scrap steel.

The brother with the one girder would happily have paid for it, but it couldn't be known that he was using it for an illegal church. When this "acquisition" was discovered, the case came up before the works management, and the Party took an interest immediately. Using a single girder for an illegal church was much worse than purloining enough to build a whole bridge. He was arrested, lost his job and had to pay a fine that amounted to a whole year's salary. Naturally he couldn't pay this, so he was thrown into prison. As a so-called "saboteur" he was badly mistreated and humiliated every day by being made to do the dirtiest jobs. He very much regretted his theft, but it didn't help him. He was given hardly anything to eat. The other prisoners would often take even this away from him, or mix it with faeces, for, after all, wasn't he a "saboteur"? In the end he became so ill as a result of harsh treatment and hunger that he died in prison.

Many others from that congregation were treated badly as well. Some individuals were held in custody for weeks at a time. They had to endure horrendous interrogation and torture. The half-finished church was crushed by bulldozers and a warning notice for all secret churches was put up in its place.

My mother didn't like going into the "gospel cave" (as we called it) in the mountainside in Nanyang because she couldn't dance there. During one period when my father was with us for quite a while, she had started to learn worship dancing. She had seen it once at the home of another Christian lady and it had caught her interest straight away. To start with it looked rather awkward and funny, and it wasn't spiritual enough for some of the Christians. But over time she became very good at it and even gave dancing lessons. Worship dance gradually became a fixed part of our meetings – only not in the gospel cave, because there simply wasn't enough room.

When the political climate eased and we were again able to meet openly, there were even dance displays at public festivals.

Although our village was always very poor, we still enjoyed celebrating festivals. The Moon Festival on 15 August – according to the Chinese lunar calendar – was one of the high points. It's a festival for the whole family. People eat special food together, including moon cakes, which are a mixture of beans, meat, nuts, and chocolate baked in shortcrust pastry. People celebrate in the streets and wish everyone they meet long life and happiness. Then they of course gaze up at the full moon, which is particularly easy to see on this date. They see the shape of a lady with a hare, and everyone swoons at the beauty of this lady. The moon unites people with relatives who can't be at home on this day, because they are also looking up at the moon and celebrating.

Dancing also takes place at the New Year Festival, our most important celebration. It marks the beginning of the New Year according to the Chinese calendar – the year of one of the twelve holy animals: dragon, snake, horse, ram, monkey, rooster, dog, pig, rat, ox, tiger, or hare.

According to the Western calendar, the New Year Festival takes place between 21 January and 21 February. Chinese people in these countries also get together with their family and eat delicious food. This includes fish, but you aren't permitted to eat it because the words for "fish" and "luck" sound quite similar. Superstition certainly plays a big part in all this, but we Christians didn't let this put us off, and joined in heartily with the celebrations.

People exchanged gifts of money in red envelopes. In our community we also gave each other gifts, only our red envelopes contained a word from the Bible or a bookmark. The red colour was very important, although it came from the belief that evil spirits could be scared off by that colour. In the same way, then, they must be afraid of the red blood of Jesus, who gained the victory over evil and sin with his blood.

Around Labour Day on 1 May and on the National Day on 1 October there were street parties and folk festivals all over China. People enjoyed the dance displays put on by my mother and her group, even though they were dancing at festivals put on by Communist China. The dance groups tried to convey the gospel by means of their dancing, though this wasn't clear at first sight. But if people asked questions, we could speak personally about the gospel, and then they could understand the various movements in the dances.

Many evangelists and preachers were guests in our house in more peaceful times. We didn't have much to eat, it's true, but there was always enough for the visitors. Sometimes I had to go to bed with a grumbling stomach because we had yet another preacher staying. When that happened I would often get up during the night to see if there were any leftovers, but there seldom were.

But the guests did give me gifts in other ways. They prayed for me and blessed me. Many of them prayed that I should become a powerful preacher, and I wished this for myself more and more too.

When I was eleven years old, I attended a Bible school that my father was running. After the lessons we were sent out in groups to preach and evangelize. The long walks were strenuous for me at that age, so some of the older ones used to carry me on their shoulders. We made the long stretches over fields, through thick forests, and over mountain ridges seem shorter by singing and praying as we went.

Having arrived in one small village, we were greeted with a sumptuous meal. The people there were poor and didn't have enough for themselves, but the visit of the Bible scholars was a huge encouragement to them, and they celebrated it with us. One elder asked me to preach in front of seventy farmers. I was only eleven, and didn't know what to say.

The other Bible scholars encouraged me too. They had confidence in me because I was the son of Brother Yun. I went into the bedroom and hid myself under the blanket. With my eyes closed, I opened the Bible and prayed that the Lord would let me find a good text. I opened the Bible up several times in the Old Testament, but couldn't say much about any of those stories. After many attempts I found a story on which I could preach. It was in John's Gospel, chapter 4: Jesus meets the woman at the well.

The church service took place in the enclosed courtyard of a dwelling house. It had a wall round it, which was too high to see over. One narrow doorway led into the courtyard. This was locked when the congregation gathered there. The seventy men and women were very excited about what the boy would say, but first of all came songs and prayers. I know today that I didn't preach well; I rambled on incoherently about God and Jesus.

After twenty minutes came a tumultuous noise of car alarms and men's voices. They wanted to get into the courtyard. As the door was locked, they kicked it in and made a forced entry. They were plain-clothes policemen, and they grew very angry when they saw so many Christians together. They cut down the clothes line with their knives and began to tie the people up with it. The man in charge kept shouting: "Who's the leader of this counter-revolutionary rabble?"

I was naturally seized by a dreadful fear. I knew of course how they treated Christians. My father had told us terrible things about what he had been through and also about other Christians who had been tortured and killed because of their faith. I trembled and prayed for Jesus to protect me.

It was somehow clear to me that one day I too would have to suffer for my faith, but please not yet, I prayed. I was still too afraid of pain and prison. The test had come too soon!

Suddenly I remembered a song that Nai Nai always sang: "Jesus loves me, Jesus loves me; I am hidden in his bosom." Trembling, I prayed that Jesus would take me to his bosom right now and not let me suffer yet.

Then one of the policemen came forward and spotted me. He smacked me on the bottom and said that I ought to get away. Children should not be at forbidden meetings like this. I was transported over to the door by a hefty kick up the rear.

Unsurprisingly, I ran outside immediately and disappeared.

Later on the police found out that I had in fact been the preacher, and they began to scour the village for me. But one of the families had hidden me well. Next day they took me under a cover in an ox cart to the bus stop, and even paid my fare. I arrived home safe and sound.

The congregation and the other Bible scholars had been held all night in the courtyard and interrogated. They were supposed to betray the names of other Christians and meeting places, but we had been trained never to betray another person, so many of them were beaten instead. The next morning the police drove away annoyed, without information and without the youthful preacher. But my fellow Bible scholars were taken into custody because they were from out of the area and were viewed as illegal evangelists. The sentence for this was normally three years in jail. They were held for several months with very little to eat and no decent place to sleep.

The police had also taken away the owner of the house. He was fined for letting his house be used for a forbidden meeting – or an "illegal assembly", as it was known. The names of the others from the village who had been present at the gathering were written down, and they had to live with the prospect of further trouble, especially if they were ever again caught during a raid.

Despite my fear, this experience was actually an encouragement to me. God hears our prayers. He doesn't ask more than we can bring. I now came to a decision that I would no longer try to keep out of harm's way at all costs, because I knew that the Lord helps and stands by those who travel his road. I would recount this experience of God with a full heart at other meetings from now on. In my narrative I kept back the fact that the other Bible scholars were in custody and going through a very bad time – but I was, after all, only eleven years old.

13
Forced to flee

I always went home at night, but on one particular evening I had been trying out my new bicycle and had gone to see a friend in the town. As it was by now quite late, I most unusually stayed the night at his house.

On this very night the police came to our house to arrest us all. They were really after my father again, but this time my mother was to be arrested as well. She was able to lift my sister, Yiling, over the back wall just in time so that she could run to the community leaders and seek safety with them.

Next minute the police broke down our front door and rampaged through the house searching for my father. They turned furniture over and lots of things got broken in the chaos. Our neighbours peeped in through the windows but no one had the confidence to try to stop the police – it would have been far too dangerous. Anyone who helped an enemy of the state was himself an enemy of the state. And if the police were going through our house then we must have committed some kind of crime – or so it seemed to people then.

My mother was arrested, but they didn't beat her at that point. Only later, at the police station where there were no witnesses, did they kick her, hit her with clubs and abuse her with offensive slander and accusations. They wanted to find out my father's hiding place from her. The methods of torture that they used were sadistic, but they didn't get the information they wanted. When they stuck sharp needles under her fingernails my mother screamed so loudly that it gave even the police the creeps – but they got no information anyway.

My grandmother was not arrested – she hid at the house of some friends, and later fled with us to the provincial capital. Eventually, she returned to Liu Lao Zhuang, our village, and made our house into a home once more.

I knew nothing of this police raid because I had stayed the night with my friend and gone to school the next day without a care in the world. But when I saw that my sister wasn't at school I went home to find out what was going on. The front door was partly split, hung with a chain and locked. I recognized the chain as the type that only the police used, and was guessed at once what had happened. Through the window I could see that much had been destroyed in the house. In a muddy ditch outside lay a black and white photograph of my grandfather which meant a lot to my father. Either the police had simply thrown it away or they had dropped it as they took the still-useable things from our house.

I was seized by such a sudden fear of being arrested myself that I didn't trust myself to pick up the picture, wipe it clean and put it in my pocket. Even now I can still sometimes see this precious photo lying in the mud in front of me – and think how my father would have been so pleased if I had been able to hand it to him later.

I ran quickly to the community leader's house and found my frightened and sobbing sister there.

An hour later we were on the bus heading for the town. We were fleeing from the police and all we had left were the clothes on our backs. I lost my new bike, of course, and my schoolbag had been left behind in the village. Our protectors later found a way of letting my sister and me continue with our lessons, but I never saw my beautiful bike again.

In the town there were Christians waiting for us, and they helped us to travel on to the provincial capital of Henan, Zhengzhou.

I am so grateful to these men and women for getting us out of the danger zone so quickly. If they hadn't, we would have shared the fate of many children of enemies of the state who were in custody. These children were placed in "approved schools", which had been set up partly to brainwash children into abandoning their Christian beliefs. Psychological methods were used to turn them into friends of Communism. As children are easily influenced, this process was, unfortunately, almost always successful. If their parents were later released from prison, this "treatment" had often made the children develop such a negative attitude towards them that they didn't want to go back to live with them. How dreadful it is for Christians who have been tortured for years in prison for Jesus' sake and had to go through torments of the soul, and survived all that, to find that their own children renounce them! I would never willingly have turned against my parents, but how do I know just what the authorities in such places of correction might have done to make me recant?

14

Disappointed by God

We were country children, and city life wasn't easy for us. For me and my seven-year-old sister it meant learning a new dialect, finding new friends, and standing our ground among strange children. The city was dirty and loud, and I didn't like it at all. Back in the village we had sometimes dreamed of living in the city, with big shops, well-built stone houses, and lots of cars. But now I had a long way to go before I could see a field. The park was pretty enough, but we weren't allowed to play there because the grown-ups used it as a place for practising their tai chi and taking a rest, and their concentration was not to be disturbed. It's true that there had been rubbish lying around in our village too, but here in the city every corner of the house smelled different.

In Zhengzhou we were able to live with a Christian lady, but she had only a very small apartment and was very poor. She had set up a little business selling cloth, but it didn't provide enough for even one person to live on. Now we were there too, placing another burden on her household. There was nothing for it but to go out on the streets and see if we could make some money.

So we began to collect rubbish: bottles, metal, and

paper. We could get some cash for this at the rubbish collection centre, which we could use for much-needed food and school equipment. The dirty things we had to pick up made me feel really queasy. From that time on I have had a habit of always looking at the ground in case I find coins that people have carelessly dropped.

I found the dirt, the cramped flat, and the smell of the city unbearable. In addition, we had to put up with the scorn the other pupils showed us as village children and for our peculiar dialect. And we had to conceal our Christian faith as well. All in all it became too heavy a burden for me. I got angry with God, and I felt very embittered.

"God, you have blessed my grandmother, but you've taken her away. You have blessed my father, but he is not here. You have blessed my mother, but you've also let her go to prison. You were going to bless me too, but I can't see any evidence of it. You must be a tiny, weak God. The gods of the Chinese people seem much bigger and more powerful. There are temples to these gods everywhere, but where are *you*?"

I had of course been through a lot with God, but in this city he seemed to me to have become small and ineffective. My hatred of this puny little God was so great that I decided never to become a preacher.

I understand now how it's possible for people living through terrible circumstances to be unable to believe in God's love. For me the realization came later, when I was seventeen, that even if I could hate God, he still loved me. He didn't abandon me, even when at thirteen I wanted to stop following him.

A new temptation lay in wait for me in the city – materialism. Some of the boys in my class had cassette players, CD players, and computers, all of which were totally new to me and which at first I didn't understand. Steadily the desire grew in me to possess this technology too. But it was as far away from me as the source of the Yangtze was from its delta on the Yellow Sea. It was just one more reason for being dissatisfied with God.

So that no one could link us with our father, I was even given a new name. I was now called Yang Yun. The name came from my mother, who was from a family of Yangs. It was hard for me to get used to this. When the teacher called out "Yang Yun", I either didn't react at all or responded so late that it must have been obvious that it wasn't my real name.

After three months, in 1997, my mother was released from jail. We moved again, this time to a totally new part of town. We broke off all connection with friends and also with our church community. My mother had suffered a great deal and couldn't bear the thought of going back to prison. She was desperate to spare us all from that.

In spite of our self-imposed isolation, news reached us that my father had been miraculously set free from jail. He was now lying low with some Christians in Wuhan.

We were able to visit him there, although it was very risky for all concerned. My father's reports were terrifying and inconceivable in their horror. We realized that one more spell in prison would inevitably mean death for him.

Again we moved house; it was becoming the norm for us to flee from one town to another. In the province of Shandong lived a family with whom we had been connected for three generations. We were able to go to ground with them. I am very grateful to that family for giving us security again. With their help we even got an apartment, and again we changed our names. I was now called Wang Ming Yun. Once more there was a new school system, a new dialect, and new contacts.

In spite of my dislike of the "puny" God, I still held firmly on to him. I read the Bible and prayed, though it was more intellectual than heartfelt. But remarkably, despite this, I managed to bring some other young people to faith in Jesus, and even worked with a Christian children's group.

15

A guest of the official church

During this period we maintained a connection with the Three-Self Church, telling no one that our father was a pastor of the underground church. The Three-Self Church is the official church, which has state permission to use and even build new churches. As I have said, it called itself the Three-Self Church because it had three principles: "self-determination", "self-support", and "self-propagation". It had been founded when all the foreign missionaries were forced to leave the country in 1949/50.

At that point the Christians in China were suddenly thrown back on their own resources. In order to prove that Christianity wasn't just a Western movement, the country's Christians set up their own Chinese church. The state couldn't do much about this, though it tried again and again to exercise influence over it – with varying degrees of success. The Patriotic Chinese Catholic Church functioned in much the same manner. Independent from the overseas church – thus also from the Pope in Rome – they fashioned their own Masses and consecrated their own priests. The Catholics too had an underground church, which hadn't renounced Rome and continued to belong to the worldwide Catholic communion. This didn't suit the state at all, as it would tolerate no "foreign interference", which is how it regarded the spiritual responsibility of the Pope for all Catholics.

The evangelical Three-Self Church described itself as a post-denominational church. The various denominations – Lutheran, Methodist, Baptist, Anglican, etc. – no longer existed: in the Three-Self Church all evangelical Christians were united. It was still obvious from their services what sort of denomination they had come from, but ostensibly there was just one evangelical church. The state made no moves to stop it because its informants and the fact that services were held in public showed that no subversive and revolutionary plans were being hatched there.

In the first few years after 1950 the state controlled this church strictly and even exercised a strong influence over its leading bishops. At the same time there was growing conflict with the house churches. There was mutual suspicion and betrayal. Christians on both sides ended up in prison because of false witness, and there was a lot of guilt. Luckily this time is long past, if not yet quite resolved.

The state couldn't maintain such strict control over the underground churches, and that's why it was so suspicious of them. It declared their meetings illegal and took upon itself the right to close churches at any time and to arrest collaborators and throw them into jail. Yet the house churches flourished under this pressure and persecution, and the believers were strengthened rather than frightened off. But we were now in the sights of the state police, and our family had a tough time of it in those years.

Through a series of miracles my father managed to flee to Germany in 1997, when we – my mother, Yiling, and I – were submerged in anonymity in the eastern part of China. While here we would go to the Three-Self Church service every Sunday. My faith grew gradually firmer again. I really looked forward to every service in the overfilled church! It did me good to be among cheerful Christians who had no fear of police raids, some of whom stood in the street outside the church and sang loudly without restraint! At the baptism services I was always amazed by the number of people joining the community. Sometimes there were well over a hundred at a time, mostly adults.

Once, during a Bible hour at the Three-Self Church, at which at least 500 people were present, the pastor asked the congregation what it was that we had been saved by. I wanted to answer straight away: "By faith in Jesus Christ." Yet my mother held me back, because this answer might have revealed that we were members of the underground church.

It wasn't actually dangerous to live as a Christian, and even at school they knew that I went to the Three-Self Church. But if they had discovered that we had come from the house-church movement, they would have become suspicious. "House church" is still an emotive term to this day, and many still suspect that sectarian movements lie behind it.

But within the Three-Self Church more and more openness and trust were being shown towards the Christians from the underground churches. The enmity of earlier years was a thing of the past. The respective leaders even met in secret to try to build a new relationship with one another. Yet the official Party line was that the house communities were still classified as anti-state and counter-revolutionary. So we tried not to be provocative and did not openly declare our allegiance to them.

Our contact with the house churches kept growing slowly, however. Christians from house churches would come to visit us in secret or pick us up by car. House-church meetings took place mostly in the villages in those days, though today the movement has spread just as widely in the towns.

I was even asked again to preach in the house churches. This strengthened my faith, and it often seemed to me that I was preaching to myself. When people started coming to me to have me pray for them and bless them, I knew that God had forgiven me for my disobedience and my resentment of him.

On one short secret visit to my grandmother, I realized that we were seeing each other for the last time. She no longer left her little apartment now because she had had an accident, and had broken her leg. Nai Nai had no health insurance and couldn't pay for an extended stay in hospital. So she just lay down for a long time and waited in considerable pain until her bones knit themselves back together. She was looked after by the community in our home village.

As she could no longer put her weight on that leg, Nai Nai was confined to the house. We would gladly have taken her in, but we were ourselves dependent on the help of other Christians, and frequently on the run. Later my grandmother became so ill that she put on her ornate funeral robe and simply waited for death to fetch her home to Jesus. But when she heard that her son, my father, was safe and able to live in Germany without persecution, she blossomed again, took off her funeral robe, and wanted to carry on living and praying that God would bless my father's evangelistic work. She finally died in 2000. None of us were able to be with her.

16

The exam is cancelled

My life changed completely one balmy evening in May 1999. I had had a bad day. I had rushed through a maths exam, because maths really wasn't my strong point. Feeling gloomy, I sidled along the row of houses in the dusk to reach home.

A neon sign had been put up above a new department store, and it flashed in garish colours. The red star glowed over the entrance to the Party building and a red cross crowned the tower of the town church. Because my head was full of maths, it struck me for the first time that the cross is the great plus symbol. Jesus is the plus symbol for my life, for our country, for the whole world. That was more important than maths. My heart grew a little lighter at this. The next day I would have to redo the work, and I intended to plead with the great plus symbol to let me pass the exam this time. But it didn't come to that.

As I open the door of our flat, my mum draws me quickly into the room and locks the door. With a determination that I haven't seen in her for a long time, she says: "Isaac, you've got an hour to pack your most important things in a bag. We're going to Burma; we're leaving China."

"But how come? Why? I have to resit my exam tomorrow. This evening I need to revise and swot up on formulas!"

My mother, herself feverishly busy with packing, stands up straight and places her hands on my shoulders: "Isaac, get a bag and pack everything that matters to you and that you'll need in the next few days. We're leaving in an hour. Please understand: we're leaving China!"

Leaving China? My mind goes numb; I can only feel. Feel suddenly that I am Chinese. My country, with its magnificent mountains, its mighty rivers; my country with its rice fields laid out at right angles, which gleam at first light green, then leaf green, finally golden yellow and, after the harvest, brown. I see before me the black patches in the landscape where unusable rice and maize straw is burned. I see the night-time glow of fire over these fields and I suddenly long for our village... To walk through the muddy alleys once again, to look down the well in the central square, seeking my reflection in the mirror of the water, and to sniff in the scent of the wooden maize stores. To go down to the river one more time – to see whether the aluminium bowl from our last splendid haul of fish has turned up again.

I see our ruined house and the photograph of my grandfather lying in the mud. I see myself going round the villages with Nai Nai, and the many Christians smiling at me. They are singing a song that I can't understand. Which text are they singing from?

"Hurry up; stop daydreaming," I hear my mother warn me. Reality strikes again. Flight – that means we are in danger; it means leaving my beloved China by secret routes. Though I'm not quite fourteen years old it is clear to me that leaving this sealed-off Communist country is an extremely dangerous course of action. The state has not yet let anyone out willingly, and, because my father has already fled the country, we are under particularly close observation.

Anxiety surges within me and homesickness tries to force me to stay in my own country. Mechanically I take a few items of clothing and my Bible from the shelves, and stick a few photos in the bag with the two big handles. We chose this sort of luggage precisely because if need be we could use the loops and carry it on our backs, leaving our hands free. How glad I am now that we did so!

I have to leave behind many things that mean a lot to me as a young boy: my new sports shoes, the new pocket calculator, an illustrated book about the ancient and modern wonders of the world, many religious books, and my collection of badges from the various festivals and special occasions.

Now my mum does something that surely isn't sensible – but she too is suffering the wrench of leaving. We make our way back to our own community in Nanyang. Many Christians come together in secret to bid us farewell. No one trusts themselves to sing, but they pray fervently over us and bless us. Lui Chan, one of the leaders, says to me: "When you come back you will be thirty years old, Isaac. You will have a wife and children, and you must bring them with you, as we want to see your children."

Then everything happens quickly. A brother who owns

a car drives up. Under the cover of darkness we climb in. My mother, my sister Yiling, and I settle ourselves in the back seat. Whenever people appear on the road the driver gives us a sign before we reach a street lamp and we duck down behind the front seats, my sister in particular having to crouch down low in her central position. It's difficult when another car comes up behind us, as we have to stay bent down like this for a long time.

It happens just before the next town. The police have set up a roadblock and we have to stop. As three policemen with machine guns approach our car, my mother warns us: "Don't duck; look inconspicuous." My sister trembles so much that it makes me shake too.

"Have you seen two men in prison uniform? They broke out this morning and must be on the road somewhere around here."

"No, Comrade, we haven't seen anyone suspicious," replies the driver.

One of the policemen takes a long look into the car through the open window.

"What's wrong with the little one? She's shivering all over."

My mum uses her God-given quick wits: "She's freezing because the window's open."

"Well, then, shut it and drive on carefully – and don't stop if you meet anyone on the road."

The driver murmurs to himself: "We will gladly obey *that* order" – but because the window is now closed again the policeman can't hear any more.

In the town we drive up a shabby side street into an

area where all the houses are surrounded by a high wall. The road surface is so bad that we are thrown from side to side in the car. We turn right in front of a huge mound of gravel and end up in a courtyard. The red sheet-metal doors close quickly behind us.

Here we find another car with a number plate from this town. Again there are Christians here, although it is by now 2 a.m. There is a quick break for a cup of tea and to use the toilet. Then we have to get into the other car. We drive aimlessly through the town. We've been provided with travel tickets but the train doesn't leave till the morning, and so we have to pass the time driving around. Apparently it's too dangerous to spend the night at the house of one of the Christians.

I soon notice that we are making a kind of figure of eight through the town. We have already passed the Mao memorial several times. Suddenly a motorbike comes up to us, flashing its headlight. Our driver slows down and the motorbike turns and follows us. When it has drawn level our car stops and the driver speaks briefly with the motorcyclist, thanks him and carries on with his figures of eight.

"Brother Chi says there's a police barricade on the Street of the Great Revolution. He came to warn us."

As we spot the first grey streaks of dawn, our car is driven in another direction. In a small factory yard there's a motor rickshaw waiting, which is to take us from here. There's just enough room for three people but none left for luggage, so we have to put our bags and packages on our laps, thereby forfeiting any chance of remaining upright when we go round corners – these rickshaw drivers are masters at bends and short cuts.

This adventurous companion takes us to the station, where a swarming throng has already gathered. We can be set down here unnoticed and disappear into the crowd. Before we say goodbye to the rickshaw driver he gives us the tickets and an address, which we are to make a mental note of. My mother and I study the address carefully. My nerves are so taut with anxiety that I will still recall it in years to come. It is a house on White Hill Street in Kunming.

17

The network of Christian "agents"

We soon found our train. Our places were in the compartment with hard benches. In China travellers are offered the choice of soft seats or hard ones. The latter are usually wooden or plastic benches on which four or five passengers must do their best to fit. To get a soft seat you need to have a ticket issued in your name – and obviously we couldn't order those. These seats are expensive too, because you can lie down and sleep on them. I would have liked to do that right then. My sister had actually fallen asleep in the rickshaw, in spite of its bumpy cornering.

As I hunched in my corner and the train pulled slowly out of the town, I had to smile. What we were going through was just like a thriller. I had actually read one like this once, only the police had been hunting a serious criminal who always seemed to know how to trick them.

The house-church communities had a marvellous system of mutual assistance when anyone was in trouble. I believe we were in the hands of an effective secret service. It would have been impossible for us on our own to cope with the distances or find our way through the loophole into Burma. The fares alone would have been too much for us to raise.

So we fled, and our flight went like clockwork. Everywhere we went there were Christians waiting unobtrusively to greet us, give us fresh provisions, and provide the tickets for the next stage of the journey. Not until much later did we discover that our escape had been made possible by the German charity AVC (*Aktion für verfolgte Christen und Notleidende* – Action for Persecuted and Needy Christians) and their partners in China. We wouldn't have got out of China without these people.

The landscape became more mountainous; we couldn't see very far ahead. The train snaked between deeply cut valleys. We passed steep mountainsides, wooded to their very peaks. Some of them were so steep that I had to kneel down by the window to be able to make out the top. I was sure that no one could have climbed them yet. I would gladly have got off the train and tackled the ascent, but I had grown so stiff on the long train journey that I would probably have worn myself out on such a mountain.

Suddenly it dawned on me again that I had to leave all this. Burma might well be a beautiful country too, but we would not be able to stay there. Where would our journey end? Would we ever find a new home? In Singapore, Korea, or America, maybe? Or would we be seized and thrown into a Chinese jail? Might we be separated from our mother, tormented and tortured because they wanted to get information about my father out of us? Or would we be shot while on the run? What would become of me if they shot my mother and Yiling and I alone was left alive?

What would I do then? I certainly didn't know where I could find Christians who would help me further.

What kind of language did they speak in Burma? I knew only Chinese and a few Chinese dialects.

A dreadful anxiety arose in me. It crushed me like a lead weight and I actually felt sick with fear. I prayed, but it didn't help. I breathed as if I'd just run a thousand-metre race. Sweat ran from all my pores. I had to rush to the dirty toilet to throw up. I felt like death and even thought that it might be best for me to be shot immediately. Should I jump out of the train? Should I tell the conductor what we were planning, so that everything would be over?

When I returned I saw at once that Mum knew what was wrong with me. There was a deep sadness in her eyes, but she couldn't comfort me. We couldn't even talk about my fears; there were just too many people crammed into our compartment. I longed for her to give me an encouraging word or whisper a prayer with me – but we couldn't risk it.

I sat down next to her and she laid her hand on my head. I knew that she was uttering a silent blessing over me. At this I was unable to hold back my tears, although I felt very ashamed to be crying in front of the other passengers. A Chinese boy of almost fourteen is not supposed to weep!

The other people in the compartment looked quite astonished at this; they were probably surprised because until then we had been really quiet during the journey. But my mother's quick wits came to the rescue again and she comforted me quietly with these words: "My boy, don't be sad; your grandfather is with the ancestors now, and we shall make an offering for him when he is buried."

My sister looked over at us, confused by these strange words coming from Mum's mouth, but I understood her clever evasive action and was even almost able to smile at it.

An older lady had been watching us closely for some time. She asked: "You're not from Yunnan Province, are you? You speak a different dialect. You talk like the Han Chinese from Central China."

"You're right. We come from the Province of Henan; we have a family matter to sort out in Kunming," replied my mum, trying to tell as few lies as possible.

Night fell and I lay down in the gangway, as I just couldn't sit up any longer. The wheels rattled hard against the joints in the track, and the steel floor of the carriage carried the rhythmical pounding straight to my head. The floor stank repulsively but I was at least able to lie down and stretch out my legs. My mum had taken my sister onto her lap, but she herself couldn't sleep. I hadn't seen her get any sleep on the entire journey so far – but maybe she could allow herself some rest when her children were asleep.

I am woken by a pair of feet shoving me aside in the gangway. It isn't someone needing the toilet, but officials in uniform, wanting to check the passengers' papers. Although my mother hasn't told us everything, I know that we have no official papers. Not everyone in China has their papers on them, but anyone who wants to go abroad has to have a passport. We don't have any, but at first no suspicions are aroused.

But then the police demand our papers and want to know exactly where we have come from and where we are going. Because my mum isn't able to give a clear answer, the policemen threaten to throw her off the train at the next station and say that our background will be investigated carefully at the police station.

Then the older lady opposite intervenes and explains effusively to the police that my mother is only a simple woman and that her circumstances are poor. She is a respectable farmer's wife and wants only to bury her father in Kunming and then travel home again. The children are so upset by the death of their grandfather that they already have enough of a weight of sorrow to bear. The policemen should show themselves to be on the side of the simple people, as they had been in Mao's time, and should not be pestering respectable farmers, who work the land for everyone's benefit.

"Imagine that *your* father had just died. You would have fog in your brain too and would want people to leave you in peace. So leave us alone here and do what you have to do somewhere else!"

The officers are visibly impressed by this, and clamber away over the suitcases, packages and people that are blocking the gangway. So that's what angels look like, I think to myself. My mum nods over at the lady, who winks back at her while a hint of a smile plays around her lips.

18

In a Chinese Volkswagen among buffalo carts and goats

Early the next day we arrived in Kunming. A brother from one of the house churches accompanied us through the city. White Hill Street was not near the centre so we had to take a taxi and drive for half an hour out of this teeming city. I saw at once that the street deserved its name. The houses were built on a slope, and its chalky soil shimmered pale between the turf, gardens and fruit trees.

A foreign missionary lived here, who worked to all intents and purposes as a teacher and could do her mission work only in secret. She considered our flight to be very dangerous. Her anxiety was so great that she asked us to leave her house, even though the sun had not yet set. I realized yet again that we had undertaken a very risky journey, though so far everything had gone well.

Yet the most difficult part of our flight would be getting over the border between China and Burma. What was lying in wait for us there? Would we be seized? Were we heading for prison, torture, and pain, or for freedom? Would we see our father again, and would I ever come back to my homeland? I had thought that Kunming was right on the border, so the fact that we still had another 400 miles or so to cope with came as an immense shock to me.

We slept in a park, under a big white rock. Early the next morning, as there were no more trains going in the direction of Burma, we had to get a taxi. We were to be in its driver's company for a whole day. Would he notice anything?

We travelled through a magical world of mountains. The famous "stone forest" lay near Kunming. We had heard about it in school and seen pictures. It was a vast area of curiously shaped limestone formations. Each rock had a traditional name, but the fissures, passageways, and caves that one could visit there were even more romantic. Castles with turrets and flights of steps surrounded by water, grottoes full of mythical creatures and rocks that looked like people at work – all this created by nature by means of erosion and the convulsions of the earth. The stone forest was a tourist magnet for visitors from all over the world.

Yet no matter how hard I tried, I couldn't make out any of it. The engine of the Chinese Volkswagen hummed monotonously as the driver steered it skilfully through the many curves of the mountain road. There were mountains on both sides now, higher than any I had ever seen. Some of them were between 9 and 12,000 feet high. The taxi driver knew many of their names. Because I showed an interest, he told us a lot about the flora and fauna and the people who lived in the seclusion of the mountains. Many minorities lived here – small populations that had integrated into Chinese society. They were permitted to maintain their own language and customs, but naturally had to abide by the law of the land, and alongside their own dialect their children learned Mandarin Chinese. But their special rights included being exempt from the state's one-child policy, so of course they could have more than one child. The driver also told us that they had splendid and gloriously colourful traditional costumes, but didn't wear them on normal working days.

We saw villages that looked even poorer than our huts in Liu Lao Zhuang. Many were made only of clay, and because of rain and bad weather they had become crooked or had partly collapsed. As we passed through yet another such village, we were stopped by a funeral procession that was making its way along the road to the edge of the village. Some of the people were wearing their ornate traditional dress, but all had a white cap or hat. White is the colour of mourning. The body had been wrapped in a cloth and laid on a two-wheeled cart. In front of it they carried simple bunches of flowers and a large bright rosette made of coloured paper and flowers. Typical Chinese funeral music sounded from the village loudspeakers.

We were seeing hardly any cars now. On the roads, which were getting rougher and rougher, were buffalo carts and teams of goats instead. Many people carried their loads on a pole slung over their shoulders. We could clearly see how these poles sagged like a spring with each step the person took.

One farmer was driving his goats in front of him, so close that they could almost have climbed into the car.

As they wandered across the road our alert driver had to brake so hard that we almost hit the front seats. The farmer muttered threats at him nevertheless, and chucked mud at the car.

This was quite normal, the driver told us, because the people around here didn't like cars. Maybe they were also a bit envious of this speedy form of transport, seeing that they had to be on the road day in, day out with their ponderous carts.

What did pass us more and more often, though, were military vehicles – smoke-belching stinking trucks carrying soldiers or loaded with tarpaulin-covered weapons. We started every time when, beyond a bend, one of these monstrous lorries took up the entire road. Our driver was often forced so close to the edge that he preferred to stop and let the truck rumble past. At one point we couldn't go any further because the wheels were spinning. The driver was naturally concerned about his valuable car, but with the help of an ox cart we made it back onto the road again.

Our goal was the border town of Yingjiang. There were three or four checkpoints on the way there. Passing these was always a bit nerve-wracking, but we had the address of a hotel in Yingjiang and also confirmation that we had booked a room there. This was yet another achievement of the house-church "secret service". We would have been under suspicion without this information, and would probably have been sent back or even arrested. What was a woman with two children and luggage doing in the border region?

But in spite of this there were always questions and unexplained delays as we journeyed on. In the end it was our driver who exerted pressure and through his harsh words ensured we continued our journey. We had brought a small amount of money for just such occasions, but had to be sparing with it because anyone who paid too high a bribe was clearly planning something forbidden. That's why, when it seemed that we weren't going to get any further, my mother finally asked what the policemen really needed. "A kilo of meat and a bottle of brandy." We of course had neither, but their cost – around 150 yuan – was enough to open the barrier.

19

We leave China

In Yingjiang there was a pastor who looked after us. He too said that our plan was dangerous and that the border with Burma was not only well watched but also hard to cross. But, full of hope, we felt that we ought to try it as soon as possible.

It was around midday on 10 May 1999. Well-informed members of the church community knew that the soldiers had a sleep around this time because being on guard duty staring at a sluggish river was very boring for them.

The pastor drove us to the river, where he had arranged for a boat to meet us. He had to leave us on our own from this point. My mother grasped the oars and my sister and I lay down in the bottom of the boat. A woman alone in a boat was less suspicious – she might be a farmer's wife, a herb collector or a shepherdess going to look after her animals.

We reached the far bank unharmed and unnoticed and climbed out. Then we had to push the boat back into the water so that the current would carry it away and cover our traces.

But this wasn't the border itself; we were still in Chinese territory. The river that formed the actual border lay hidden a few hundred metres away, running between high banks.

We made our way through thickets and reed beds. The last stretch before the water involved sliding under an eroded overhang. With extreme caution, my mother then stepped into the water and peered along both riverbanks, but couldn't see anything that might spell danger for us. Apparently there were no soldiers stationed here on the river, or maybe they were lying dozing in the reed beds.

Then my mother takes us by the hand. We have our bags on our backs because it is safer that way, even though the handles cut painfully into our shoulders.

The first few steps out of the reed bed are terrifying: suddenly we are visible from all sides. I'm still thinking that we should have waited in the reeds till nightfall and I hesitate – but we don't dare speak.

But my mum draws me forward with great energy. The water gets deeper and deeper. The riverbed is relatively level, and we can feel a few stones with our feet. I bang my shinbone painfully against a big stone that I haven't seen because of the murky water. I am almost tipped over by this, and with my heavy bag on my back I would have gone under, but my mum grasps me and pulls me ever onwards. The water is up to my chest and up to my sister's neck.

My mother gives her a piggyback and struggles towards the far bank. She seems to be consumed by one sole aim: forwards, across, and into the safety of the thicket.

The water grows calmer again and the current slackens

off. Just a few more yards and we'll be safe.

Then we hear men calling out behind us – Chinese voices. My mum prays loudly for protection and that the blood of Jesus will keep us safe.

Again there is a shout, but no shots are fired.

Not one of us dares to turn round.

As we reach the bank and run into the reeds, water pours from all over our bodies, and our bags have scooped up plenty of it too, but we are safe. Whether the calls of the Chinese men were aimed at us, whether they were soldiers or farmers in their fields, we don't know – and it doesn't matter any more.

We battle on for a few more feet through the undergrowth and the loose branches that have caught fast in the bushes at the last high tide, until we come to the embankment. Here we crouch in a hollow for a moment and give thanks to our God.

My mum cries and hugs and kisses us over and over again. We can sense that the crazy tension has loosened its grip on her.

What do *I* feel? I am hungry, my shin is smarting, and I want to put some dry trousers on. But somehow the tension has lessened for me too, and I just want to live like a normal person again.

But when we open our bags, not much has stayed dry inside them. There's nothing to eat either. It occurs to me that our escape is not yet over.

20
In Burma

The pastor in Yingjiang had told us that we should simply keep going straight ahead. "Eventually you'll find a road on your left. After about an hour you will reach a village. There's a small church, which is easy to spot. The sisters there know you're coming and will guide you from there."

But reaching the road in the first place turned out to be a form of survival training. Even getting up the embankment was tough enough. The river had undercut the bank so much that you could shelter from a downpour in the hollow it made. So we tried to climb up from several other places. Easier said than done. We kept slipping back until we finally found a place where we could do it. In the meantime we had become encrusted in sticky mud and sand.

How exactly were we supposed to keep going straight ahead when the undergrowth was tangled and near-impenetrable? Old trees had fallen and made direct forward progress impossible. Yet my mother sang out loud and fought her way through for us. Her relief was both visible and audible.

My sister had trouble staying on her feet in such terrain, and I was hungry, really starving. It wasn't fair of me to accuse our mother of not having packed anything for us to eat. Then I noticed that she had left the path that led to the road and pushed her way through to a tree like no tree I had ever seen before. Broad, metre-long leaves hung down from it, all growing from a crown about three metres above the ground. On one side hung a thick bunch of bananas, which ended in a reddish-brown blossom. My mother wanted to pick these fruit but they were too high up. She called us to her. I hoisted my sister onto my shoulders and she was then able to reach the bananas. She managed to pull some down. They were still green, but to me they tasted better than any banana I had ever eaten.

Then we returned to the path we had beaten down. We battled through this wilderness for about two more hours, till the thicket finally thinned and we could make out an unpaved road. My mother's dress hung in tatters about her, and my trousers were ripped.

Walking on this road was like deliverance for us. We were finally able to put one foot in front of the other and no longer had to fight our way forward using our hands and our whole bodyweight. Now we children joined in with our mother's songs of gratitude and sang gospel songs, which were good to march to. As we walked, our clothing gradually dried out, until we were surprised by a shower of rain. We tried to take shelter under a big deciduous tree, but it shook so much that it gave us no protection.

My mum had managed to rediscover her sense of humour, declaring: "Now we're in God's big washing machine, so the sand and the mud will be washed off.

We'll be coming back into civilization soon, so we need to be clean for that."

It wasn't cold, even though evening was approaching. We had already noticed that it got dark here in the south much more quickly than where we came from. But, according to the pastor from Yingjiang, we shouldn't have much further to go.

The rain ceased as suddenly as it had started. We trekked on along the sodden and squelchy road and soon began to feel that our clothes were drying again.

My mother wasn't keen to enter the village in daylight because, despite the rain's efforts at laundry, we appeared quite poverty-stricken, and even pitiful. Darkness had fallen before we reached the village. Within ten minutes all was black, but through the dark trees on both sides we could still easily make out the pale swathe of road.

Suddenly a car approached us. With headlights on full beam it drove up and stopped next to us. We gripped each other's hands in fear. What did this mean?

As the car door opened, a man spoke to us in good Chinese and asked if we were the family of Brother Yun.

We were a bit disconcerted by this, as we had been using false names for so long that we had almost repressed the fact that we were the Liu family.

"Yes, we have come over the border and are looking for Christians in the next village," answered my mother.

"You're in the right place, then. We have been waiting for you and were worried in case we had somehow missed you." The man's voice was so warm and friendly that we knew we were now truly in good hands. We climbed into his car and he turned it round. It wasn't much further to the village.

I had always imagined Burma to be a rich country, because it wasn't Communist. But this village was at least as poor as the villages at home in Henan. The huts had straw roofs and there was no colour anywhere. Even the church, in which we were to sleep that night, was very simple. Its benches were so narrow that I preferred to lie on the floor. But before we could get ready for sleep, some of the church members came to greet us.

One lady brought a big bowl of warm water, one man a roast chicken. There were also fruits of different kinds, many of which were new to me. But before we could wash and begin to eat, my mum wanted to praise God with the whole congregation. We sang hymns, read some psalms and prayed – including in our prayers all persecuted and imprisoned Christians in China and everywhere else in the world.

In China we had never prayed that the persecution would cease, only that God would give us strength to bear all the oppression and the suffering. Now we saw it through different eyes. We had escaped from the persecution and now wanted our brothers and sisters to be freed from it as well. One brother from the community said to us that my father had reached Germany and was now safe. My sister wanted to know whether we could go to Germany. She wanted very much to see our father and be with him again.

My mum stroked her hair and explained to her: "Germany is so far away that we can't go there yet. We can't afford the journey. But maybe your father will come back and we'll be able to meet him soon." She would not have believed that another two years would pass before this happened.

We left this village with its friendly people for a place in the north of the country. There we were taken in by a Chinese Baptist school. We were relatively safe on the school premises. It wasn't uncommon for the Burmese police to arrest Chinese people who had no papers and have them deported back to China. That would have been the worst thing that could happen to us.

For this reason our mother didn't at first want us to go into the village and attend the normal school. In the Baptist Bible school there were around seventy to a hundred pupils from all parts of Burma, and also some from abroad. Some of these were refugees from China or children of former refugees. Some of them wanted to get an education so that they could one day re-enter China illegally. Their aim was to work as missionaries in the house churches. But most of them wanted to work among Chinese people in free countries and bring them the good news of Jesus.

Many millions of Chinese people live in other Asian countries, often speaking the language of their host country too badly to allow them to join Christian communities there. Hence there is a great need for Christian teaching in these countries, one of which is Burma.

There was also a normal Burmese school in the same place as the Bible school. Many Chinese studied here. The children of the teachers and missionaries stood to gain a good education. I did quite well in this school, and never let on that I needed to retake my maths exam. I realized that our Chinese education had been quite good. Even *I* was good at maths here. Yet to start with it wasn't easy to feel at home in this new class. For one thing I couldn't understand a word of this language that was so different from Chinese.

The meanest of the pupils nicknamed me "the one who came in from the mud". Some of them were themselves the descendants of refugees, but no one had made it over the border for some years. Apparently it was regarded as totally impossible to get out of Communist China, and so not all of them believed my story. They were even suspicious of me because I had lived in a Communist state before our flight. So I tried hard to prove myself an honourable Christian and a good friend.

I was also much further on in my faith than the boys in my class. Many of their parents were in contact with the Baptist school, but they had never been through difficulties and hostilities because of their faith. Because my faith was so important to me and I gave so much time and effort to it, I was soon given my old nickname again: "little Jesus". But this was now a positive thing to me, rather than a cause for annoyance. There was a sizeable Baptist congregation here, in which I was soon taking an active part. It was fascinating to be able at last to go to church services without fear and to talk openly to everyone about Jesus.

21
My friend Ming

Shi Ming sat next to me in school. He was a year older than me, as the class consisted of boys aged from fourteen to seventeen. His parents had been living there for some time because his father had a good job with a company that was drilling for oil in the area. But his father had abandoned the family, and his mother now had to cope with five children on her own. Ming was the eldest and was responsible for all the heavy work at home. I would sometimes help him with this. When his younger siblings were impressed by the fact that we could repair the roof or dig out a tree root, it made me feel very proud. I hadn't really ever done any physical work before, so I thought it was great to be able to do something useful with my hands.

Ming wasn't a Christian but a Buddhist, like the rest of his family. He didn't go to the temple very often, but sometimes his mother insisted that he accompany the others to light some incense sticks.

I went with them once and was amazed by how mechanical and impersonal the ceremony was. The family bought the incense sticks outside the temple. Mrs Shi exchanged some paper money, which she then offered to the ancestors. She burned the money in an incense bowl and murmured some Buddhist verses as she did so. Ming and his siblings lit the joss sticks and bowed before the gleaming golden Buddha. They didn't wait for the sticks to burn up but stuck them in a bowl of sand along with countless others.

It was clear to me that it didn't mean that much to Ming, but I didn't ask him about it.

He had no real opinion on religious matters: "I do it because my mother wants me to and because our family has been doing it for generations."

He didn't want to know about my Christian faith either. Whenever I wanted to say something to him about Jesus he blocked it at once: "Don't bother me with your Jesus. I only believe in what I can see, and in pretty women." He had a real weakness in this area. Many of the local girls had already been his girlfriends, but none stuck with him. Maybe his intentions were not serious, and he was just boasting with his stories of these girls.

I was at his house one day and we went into his room. He slept alone in the attic room, which had no gables but was like a balcony with a pitched roof. He said he wanted to show me something that he was sure would interest me as a man. Ming reached under his mattress and brought out some magazines.

I was shocked, nauseated, and at the same time magically attracted. They were foreign pornographic magazines, which he had found among his father's abandoned work papers. I had never seen such things before. I would never have imagined that such pictures could be taken.

I couldn't get those images out of my mind. I kept seeing the scenes for half the night, and I knew it was a sin. Only when I asked Jesus for purity and clarity of thought did I slowly find peace. I thought hard about my homeland and let images of it pass before my inner eye: the bend of the river, the broad maize fields, the paths between the rice fields, and the houses in which the church community had met. The paths I had taken with my grandmother, and the roads I had ridden down on my new bike. Oh, my lovely bike – and with that sigh I must have finally fallen asleep.

Next day I told Ming that I thought his magazines were awful. I didn't care now what he thought of me. I also told him that I had done penance in the night and regained my inner peace.

He didn't dismiss this, as I had expected. Instead he asked in surprise: "Is it really that simple, that you just regret something and it's all OK again?"

I replied: "No, it doesn't come from us, but when Jesus forgives our sins, they are done with. Only then can we breathe and live freely again."

"If that is really the case, then I need your Jesus for many things in my life." We climbed together up the hill that cut the village off from the north, and I told Ming about Jesus. For the first time he really listened to me, asking questions if I spoke too quickly about things that were totally alien to him.

I told of Jesus' death on the cross, and that he died for us. I told him how I felt a whole new love for Jesus, who had taken everything that was bad about life on himself, purely to save us human beings. He did it for me and for Ming.

I could tell from Ming's rapt attention that he was very moved by the fact that Jesus really loved him. And then I told him that Jesus had died because of our sins. We were no longer punished for our mistakes, because the punishment had already been borne – with a great work of suffering, pain, blood, and tears.

"If you tell Jesus now that you are sorry for all your sins and that you will gladly hand them over to him, then he will hear you and you will be free of them. It's as if you have just taken off a dirty old shirt – and he will give you a new white holiday shirt."

"Yes, Isaac, that's what I want," said Ming, slowly and deliberately.

"Ming, we'll pray together now, and you can tell Jesus in silence all the bad things you've done, all the things that hurt other people and offended God." I knew that it was always more honest to bring our sins to God out loud, but I was worried that some of the sins from Ming's life might, if expressed in words, mess me up again. I suspected that he might have done things with girls that I just wouldn't want to know about.

So I began to pray: "Jesus, Lord of the whole world, you bled on the cross for our sins. You went to your death so that we would not have to face eternal death. Thank you that you are stronger than Satan and all our guilt. You did all this because you love us – more than any person can ever love us. You love Ming too and died for him as well. Please listen now as he asks you for forgiveness."

Then I gave Ming a nudge so that he would pray for himself.

"Jesus, I don't know you, but Isaac knows you, and he doesn't lie. You really exist and I believe that you love me too. But I am a bad person. I've committed so many sins, which you didn't want me to do. I have now realized that all that was wrong, but you are the one God, who can take it all away from me."

"So, Ming, now tell Jesus everything that you want him to forgive you for," I encouraged him.

"Do you really mean that I have to tell him *everything*? I'm ashamed of it before God."

"Yes. He knows it all already, but he wants you to separate yourself from it, and for that you need to pick it up once more and throw it away."

"OK, I'll do it, but quietly."

"Yes, it's better that way," I replied with relief.

All around us was silence. Far away I could hear a dog barking. I prayed softly that Jesus would now pour out his love on Ming. After what seemed a long time I said: "Great, so now I can pronounce you forgiven."

"Wait a minute, I haven't finished yet," was Ming's reply. After a bit more time he asked: "And what if I have forgotten something? Perhaps I don't even know all my sins."

"But God will know them, and if you really want to belong to him from now on, they will be forgiven too."

Then I took my little Bible out of my pocket and read him verses 8 and 9 of the first chapter of the first epistle of John: "If we claim to be without sin, we deceive ourselves and the truth is not in us. If we confess our sins, he is faithful and just and will forgive us our sins and purify us from all unrighteousness." I knew these verses off by heart, of course, but I thought it would be better for Ming to hear them direct from the Bible, so that God himself was speaking these wonderful words to him.

"And now say these words after me: Lord Jesus Christ, I need you. Up to now I have ruled my own life and have kept falling into sin. Thank you for forgiving me. Now I give you my life, with body, soul, and spirit; with past, present, and future. Become the master of my life and change me in whatever way you will. Amen."

Line by line Ming spoke the words after me, and he really meant them.

Afterwards we embraced each other and were both incredibly happy. I had led someone to Jesus, and Ming had found the best master for his life. We ran down the hill laughing and jumping. As we passed the Buddhist temple, Ming stopped suddenly.

"My mother shouldn't come to the temple any more either. Isaac, tell her about your Jesus in our own house!"

"Why should I?" I asked. "Tell her yourself about *your* Jesus!" And we laughed again like little boys who had just thought up a good prank.

As we said goodbye outside the Bible school where I still lived with my mother and Yiling, Ming said: "Isaac, please call me Brother Ming now. I know it sounds funny, but I want it to remind us always that we belong to the one good Father."

The next day he brought me a box full of magazines

and other things, such as amulets, which he asked me to burn. I was so eager to do it that I set the whole box on fire at once. I didn't want to touch the magazines even once more.

What I didn't know was that Ming had also taken the opportunity to dispose of a few fireworks. The box now exploded, showering the whole area with burning fragments, and I had to jump backwards and forwards putting out the scattered conflagrations.

22

Reading and yet
more reading…

At school I was elected class representative, which was a great distinction seeing that I had been the last to join the class. Being class representative was a high honour in the Burmese school system. The class representative functioned as a kind of judge in all disputes – even those involving teachers. I was also consulted when it came to making decisions about timetables, outings and marks.

Whenever I wasn't with Ming, I was studying. I knew that I would be expected to undertake many tasks, so I started to learn English. We had had lessons in our middle school in Henan, but I hadn't been interested in this subject then. What would I do with a foreign language in our country, which already had so many different dialects? But now I was eager to learn this language.

I also started learning the guitar, which wasn't as easy. My fingers wanted to do everything but touch the right strings and the right frets. I had barely managed to get them on the correct strings before I had to alter my hand position. Only the prospect of accompanying the worship leader at our services gave me the energy to carry on. Earlier than I should have, I took my guitar with me to the services. Everyone was amazed that I could play this instrument – for that seemed to be the impression I had given them.

But the first few songs were a real disgrace. The congregation sang far too fast for my ability. I had scarcely got one position right before they were off into the next passage, and it sounded weird and out of tune. Yet their patience with me was exemplary. The tempo was drastically slowed and for a while we sang the only two songs that I was half able to play! After a few weeks we got used to each other and the tempo became more acceptable.

My interminable practising got on my mum's nerves, but I simply replied: "Just be grateful that I'm not playing the drums!"

It was during this period that I began to read extensively. I devoured every Christian book that I could get my hands on. As we lived in the Bible school I had unlimited access to every room, including the library. It housed an unfathomable wealth of books. I was often to be found there at midnight, still reading for all I was worth. Whenever a book went missing from the shelves it could be found in my room. This wasn't actually permitted, but in my pressing need for knowledge I overlooked this detail. Pretty soon there was a saying going round the Bible school: "If there's a book missing from the library, just ask Isaac."

I joined in with the lessons in the Bible school as often as my regular school duties allowed. I was very enthusiastic about the parts of the curriculum that dealt with different cultures. I learned many interesting details about foreign peoples and customs. For instance, I hadn't known that missionaries must first get to know the culture of the people they are working with, so that their message is not misunderstood and does not harm anyone.

At weekends I was often off on trips with the other Bible school students. In this way I got to know this impressively beautiful country and gained practice in evangelistic activities. These included not just preaching but practical help too. So I learned how to bind minor wounds, lance boils, and administer eye drops. We helped out with farm work as well, for instance once when a village was badly affected by a flood, and we would chop wood for older people who could no longer manage it themselves.

Teaching children was my particular passion. My guitar was useful here because many children had never seen such a thing. When the children came to our public events they were usually fairly well dressed, but on the streets they often ran around in tattered shirts.

I also went into the poor people's homes and was horrified by the primitive conditions in their huts. There were some children who were living by themselves, either because the parents had died or because the parents had simply chased their sons and daughters out of the house. This happened more often here than I had been used to in China. These children were then reduced to begging or stealing. We usually spent as much time as possible with them, and it made us happy to be able to give them something to eat. They would cling on to us, but we couldn't take them with us. Later, with my father, I was able to build orphanages for these children in Burma, which we still regularly visit and support.

Many visitors came to the Bible school, which gave me the opportunity to meet several well-known evangelists. When the teachers introduced me, these visitors were all amazed to meet the son of the renowned Brother Yun. Later on I came to resent this, because I was Isaac Liu, and not just the son of Yun Liu. I had my own life to live and didn't always want to be defined by my father.

Yet on the other hand I longed for my father. How was he getting on? We had not had any direct news from him; only via other Christians did we know that he was still in Germany, seeing that it was German brothers and sisters in the faith who had made his departure possible. But where *was* Germany exactly?

I busied myself in the library and found that it was one of the little countries of far-distant Europe. Our Chinese symbol for Germany suggested that many good-hearted people lived there, but was that really true? For I had also heard that the Germans had started two world wars and that their former leader, Hitler, had committed many appalling atrocities.

People in China have a better opinion of Germany than they do of England and France, because the latter two humiliated China and ruined the country economically. Although the Germans had been a colonial power in the country, it was only for a short time. My grandfather had always spoken well of the Germans. And now my father was there. Would we too travel to this distant land, or would my father come here to Burma? I could quite well imagine that. The country was beautiful, but amid the poverty and widespread paganism we could do a lot to bring the gospel to people.

23
Prisoner in a hotel

We lived in Burma for two years. It was a good and very formative time for me. Then finally, in 2001, my father was able to visit us. His plan was for us to leave Burma and travel via Thailand to Germany.

Before we left, we founded a children's home. We began with seven children and handed the management over to a teacher who was a Christian. There are 120 children living there now, and we support this work with funds raised in Germany and other European countries.

But now the time had come for us to go on the run again. My father had by now obtained a valid German passport and for security reasons did not travel with us, but went on one day ahead. We might have escaped from the Communist regime, but other countries had borders too, and differing levels of compassion for refugees. In northern Burma we were relatively safe. The Chinese Bible school was there, and many Chinese lived there anyway. But if we went south, in the direction of Thailand, we would attract more attention for being Chinese.

It just so happened that at that very time a military conflict broke out in Burma between government and rebel forces. Checkpoints were set up on the main roads and on the approaches to towns. The police were nervous and suspected every foreigner of being a potential enemy of Burma. We were certainly not terrorists or spies, but we would have to explain as much every time we were challenged – and that in a language that we hadn't really learned properly in the two years we had spent in the country.

In the city of Mandalay came the parting of the ways for my mother, Yiling, and me. My mum was taken to the border with my sister and a man from the church community. The route over the mountains and through the dense jungle was safer for them. I flew in a small plane with a companion, Pastor Yu from Singapore, to the town of Tachilek on the Burmese border.

As airports are always a revolving door for smugglers and spies, the airport security staff were vigilant. I did have a passport – but it wasn't mine! We had bought it on the black market for a hundred dollars. It belonged to a young Chinese man who had lost his life in an accident. But he looked totally different from me in the photo! We had not had time to alter the image on the passport, and it would have been very expensive in any case, as the picture would have had to be imprinted. The man had long hair and a broad face, whereas I am small-boned and at that time had very short hair. Any official who wasn't completely blind would see at first glance that it was not my passport. Yet this was my big chance to leave the country.

All I had was faith that God would let a miracle happen. I knew it was pretty cheeky to challenge God like this: a false passport, no other papers, and the tense situation on the border to boot!

When we reached the arrivals desk at the airport in the border town of Tachilek after our one-hour flight, we all had to produce our papers. Pastor Yu from Singapore stayed with me. We handed in our luggage and then waited at the customs point.

It was quite a while till we were called. One by one, we all had to step into a glass cubicle. The official would compare our details and carry out a fairly rigorous customs and passport check. Because it was taking such a long time, I had to go to the toilet. As I came out, Pastor Yu, who was already beyond the clearance desk, called out I should come quickly and that he had my passport. So I just walked straight through passport control and passed the police, who were busy with another passenger. Pastor Yu urgently grasped my arm and pulled me out of the airport building. There were some taxis outside, and before I knew what was happening he had pushed me into one of them and we were driving away as fast as possible. Once again I had experienced the help of God; it was too unreal for me to take in. Is this how modern miracles looked?

We spent the night in a basic hotel in Tachilek. I woke quite early and heard explosions going off in the town. I couldn't see anything from my window so I went over to a balcony to discover the reason for the shooting. Pastor Yu had got up too; he was full of unease. But I was curious about what was going on, so I climbed onto the hotel's roof terrace and saw that people were shooting from behind the town towards the mountains. Rocket-propelled grenades sped on their fiery paths, and after each explosion clouds of black smoke went up. The thunderous sound rolled around the landscape some four or five seconds after each missile had gone off.

It was war, then. It was a riveting spectacle and I could scarcely tear myself away from the images before me. Then Pastor Yu came onto the roof terrace in a state of anxiety and wanted me to come down.

At that very moment a missile whistled past me and struck the hotel's satellite dish. Pastor Yu shouted: "Get down, Isaac! You're in their sights."

I crawled on my stomach to the staircase that led to the hotel and which offered me safety. Again we heard a powerful detonation over in the mountains. I was suddenly forced to think of the many people who might be dying out there. Whose house would be turned into a pile of rubble by the shots, and who was bleeding and screaming in the dirt? Later, in Germany, friends would show me video games that featured just such things. But it was no game to me. Those video games always brought back the images of Tachilek.

Our journey was postponed indefinitely because of the war that had suddenly encircled us. We remained in the hotel, most of the time in the cellar, because shots were repeatedly hitting the building. They couldn't do much damage to the concrete, but they smashed plenty of window panes, showering the interior with glass.

Venturing out onto the streets was very risky. I was sixteen years old now, and there were "employment agencies" that recruited young men as soldiers and for "rearguard duties". These manhunters were often not very choosy and roughly recruited every young man they could get their claws into. That would have been all I needed!

We sat tight for days. Some of the involuntary guests forecast that it would most likely be a year before the situation calmed down again. I was advised to rid my mind of all thoughts of fleeing to Thailand, as it would simply be too dangerous. The miserable cellar spaces in which we usually took refuge also took their toll. My whole plan suddenly seemed so crazy that my spirits sank to an all-time low.

But there was a Bible verse that kept coming back into my head during those days. It took a while for it to reach my heart: "We know that in all things God works for the good of those who love him" (Romans 8:28). So the certainty grew slowly in me again that God would help me. He had miraculously brought me this far, so surely he would find a way through this for me now.

Around midday the weapons usually fell silent – lunch was more important to the soldiers than war, and so both sides left their weapons in peace for two hours. One day, as we sat down to lunch in the hotel courtyard, the police suddenly stormed in, on the hunt for recruitable young men. The losses in the mountains were apparently so high that everyone was now to be called upon to fight in this war.

Instinctively I sprang up and ran to the other wing of the hotel, where the staircase stood empty. Fear drove my feet, and in next to no time I had reached the fourth floor, which gave access to the roof terrace. I peered over the parapet and saw that the police had not followed me, but were negotiating with an older man. Pastor Yu had fled too. He appeared later, stinking and nauseated, from inside a huge rubbish bin.

I was at least out in the fresh air on the roof, but was trapped nonetheless. It had perhaps been a rash decision to withdraw up here. If they came back, there was no way out. The best I could do would be to clamber over the other flat roof to the main building and from there try to run down the stairs. But they might run into me there too, and I would fall straight into their hands.

I suddenly noticed that the four policemen had divided into two groups and were yelling up at me: "You'd better get down here fast. You're under arrest!"

I had learned enough Burmese to understand them easily, although their posture alone would have been sufficient to convey the threat. In my anxiety I prayed: "God, either draw me up to you or make me invisible."

I had moved too conspicuously along the railings of the parapet to the main building and climbed across a level surface, so it had been impossible for them not to spot me. The police grouped together again and ran as one body towards the main building in order to seize me. As soon as they were inside, I doubled back, intending to head down the annexe stairs and somehow conceal myself behind the banisters. But just as I reached the staircase again I heard the police coming up from below. Now I was totally trapped.

Finding myself on the third floor I ran along the corridor between the hotel rooms and tried to escape into one of them. Perhaps I could jump out of a window.

During a course run by the house-church community we had once practised leaping from the second floor to the ground without getting injured.

But the doors to the first three rooms were locked. The fourth opened. I squeezed myself into a corner, hoping and praying that they wouldn't storm in. But apparently it took too much effort for the policemen to climb the stairs to the upper storeys, and I remained undiscovered.

I was reminded of my prayer on the roof: "God, draw me up to you or make me invisible." Once again he had had his hand on me.

24

Fleeing to Thailand

After a month, and on a day when no shots were being fired, Pastor Yu and I decided to risk the flight over the verdant border. Once again there was a river to cross, a fairly wild tributary of the Mekong. The Christian community's "secret service" had procured a boat for us. But I had never actually travelled in a boat like this; it was the sort you would only get into in a theme park when wearing swimming trunks. Narrow and extremely unstable, it did not impress me with its reliability.

I had only recently come across the concept of a "dugout" in a missionary report from the Amazon – this must be one of those. A boatman and Pastor Yu settled themselves on two diagonal planks. I had to crouch on the floor in the bow of the boat, but was at least able to hold on firmly to both sides of it. The current of the river made this a necessity. I was soon sitting in a continuous spray of water.

I watched in fascination as the boatman moved the boat against the waves with his one paddle so skilfully that they could not overturn us. We were driven a long way downstream, but nevertheless slowly gained the far bank. The boatman had obviously judged it well, because a small town came into view on the other bank. Admittedly, as we neared the embankment we could also see many uniformed men standing there: Thai police in their brightly coloured jackets and helmets.

They had seen us coming some time ago and stared suspiciously over at us. Some took their guns from their holsters. But our boatman let us drift a bit further and steered in towards another group of men, who were waving to us from behind a boathouse. I saw that some of them were Europeans. They were members of AVC *(Aktion für verfolgte Christen und Notleidende* / Action for Persecuted and Needy Christians), whom I was encountering here for the first time. The police ran along the bank in order to reach us at the same time as this group. But we got there a moment quicker, and one of the "long-nosed ones" sprang over to me, held out a red passport and cried: "Isaac, take this! You're a German now!"

The police checked our papers and were amazed by this Chinese German who had just arrived by boat and understood no German. But everything was in order: the passport had been issued by the German embassy and the photo showed – this time for real – Isaac with a smile on his face. (Where the embassy got that picture of me from, I have never discovered.)

These police wanted to know more, however, so Pastor Yu recounted the story of my flight from China. The policemen found it hard to believe. It just wasn't possible to get out of China.

"Now, because of the war, you can't even get to the border, and the Burmese are shooting anything that moves. Not even a mouse can get over that border at the moment." The European leader of the group supplemented this with a word from Jesus: "What is impossible with men is possible with God."

Now we had to go by jeep to Bangkok. The driver explained to us that we would have to stop at many checkpoints. He had lost a lot of time on the journey to the border from Chiang Rai because the Thai government was very nervous of the ongoing war in the border region.

Yet there was not even one roadblock, and, after an eight-hour journey through marvellous mountain scenery and lush tropical vegetation, we arrived in Bangkok.

At the German embassy there were still a few things to sort out – forms of every size, just as people had always said about the Germans. They were right!

But they were friendly to me, and kept on calling other officials who wanted to see the refugee from China. Of course they were all speaking German, and my prior knowledge of that tongue was limited to "*Guten Morgen*" and "*eins, zwei, drei, vier*". My English wasn't good enough to hold a conversation in either, but Paul Hattaway, Christian and China expert, helped me to fill in all the forms, applications, declarations, and lists. Pastor Yu travelled back immediately from Chiang Rai to Burma. I am so grateful to him for being so committed to me and thereby risking his life for me. May God bless him for it!

At Bangkok airport I met my mum and Yiling again. They had had an eventful border crossing themselves.

Their companions had led them along country roads to Thailand, although "roads" was definitely not a fair description. For one whole night they had struggled through impenetrable jungle, which their companion had to hack a way through with his machete. They couldn't wear any shoes, because the crunching noise they made on the ground might have given them away. My mother had survived this barefoot march relatively unscathed, but Yiling had sustained deep cuts. They had been through woods and mud baths and over sharp rocks. It must have been an incredibly stressful journey. My mother looked thin and drawn. Her eyes kept wanting to close. Yiling had been given new clothes that looked chic and European, but she too was exhausted and spoke barely a word. Her thickly bandaged feet were stuck in far-too-big shoes, and despite her chic new clothes she looked like a clown.

25
Lufthansa flight to Germany

As we sat in the Lufthansa Boeing 747, I forgot all my worry and insecurity. I had eyes only for the giant metal birds that were taking off ahead of us or landing on the opposite runway. This was, after all, my first time in such a huge plane.

And then we were rolling down the runway and lifting off. It was wonderful to see the ground tilting as we climbed steeply up into the sky! The stewardess served me as she would a government official, and smiled at me as though we were going to be friends. I was even allowed to choose what I wanted to eat and drink. As I didn't know the names of the drinks, I told her that I would like some of the red juice in the little bottle, like the man in front of me. She willingly poured some for me, and handed me the tumbler and the half-empty bottle, which I placed on my tray. As I tasted the juice it tingled on my tongue. I had sampled red wine for the first time in my life. It was clear to me now that I really was in a whole new world.

Next time she came down the aisle I was the first to smile at her, but she had suddenly lost interest in me and hurried to the other passengers further back. I was in the window seat, with Yiling next to me and our mother in the third seat. Paul Hattaway, who was accompanying us at the request of AVC, was on the other side of the aisle. I asked my mother: "Mum, what are you thinking now?"

She smiled at me and replied with a prayer: "God, you are wonderful. You carry us on eagles' wings and lead us out of darkness into light." Then she smiled again, closed her eyes and leaned back in her seat. At this the stewardess returned, said something to my mother, tilted her seat back, and brought her a blanket.

In Germany the first people to meet me were, yet again, policemen. They came on board the aircraft, marched purposefully up to us and asked us to disembark first. We were driven to the arrivals hall in a truck with barred windows. They spoke reassuringly to us but we didn't understand a word. It all became clear in a separated-off section of the arrivals hall, where we found German brothers and sisters from AVC waiting for us. They greeted us warmly. There was a bit more paperwork to deal with – my image of Germany was not going to be shaken that easily!

The only one missing from the reception committee was my father. We discovered that he had been arrested at the official border crossing between Burma and Thailand because he had several passports on him. This was a severe disappointment to us. Was the time of suffering still not over? We were safe now: no more persecution, no more fear, no longer restlessly fleeing from one town to another, no longer hiding away, either in the thicket by a river, or in a dustbin, or on a toilet. The German passport gave me real security, and I would have been feeling great were it not for the renewed anxiety about my father.

The AVC reception committee gave us a present of chocolate. I had never eaten this before. I had read about it in books, though, and I loved the taste from the first bite. I was disappointed to find the blocks so thin!

The Christians took us by car to Giessen, to a reception camp for refugees. I don't know how far it was because all three of us fell asleep immediately we got into the car. A great weight had fallen from our souls. It was probably the first relaxed sleep we had had in years of uncertainty … so much so that they had trouble waking us up when we got to Giessen.

After a week we were allowed to leave Giessen and travelled with permanent residence permits to Nidda, where AVC had its headquarters. I made only slow progress with my language lessons because I became active immediately in the Chinese community. I preached and led worship services. Many people were encouraged by my experiences with God to follow the Lord Jesus unconditionally here in Germany.

But I didn't want to be a preacher now. My experience of God might well have been wonderful, but I didn't have the strength to undertake such a sacrificial lifestyle. I had indeed promised God several times that I would serve him with my whole life, but now I no longer wanted that. My plans now were to go into business and earn enough money for my future wife to be able to have a decent roof over her head.

I threw myself into two German courses because the language was just so difficult for me. I therefore wasn't accepted by the business school to which I had applied. Along with my lack of German there was the fact that I had no previous knowledge of this area of study.

So I started at a vocational technical college for electronic engineering. This was meant to be the springboard for my career in business, but the first six months were a disaster. I sat there in the lectures understanding almost nothing.

Only in mathematics did I see a light at the end of the tunnel. It was a real help to me that in China we had actually had a very sound education in maths, even if I hadn't passed the first exam and the second I had been unable to take for reasons I have already explained.

I felt quite miserable. Was this my calling? Being an electrical engineer and then a businessman? Was I in the right place here? These questions made me ill at ease and preoccupied me so much that I was far too absent-minded in lessons. So I had to leave this college too.

All I had left was a plea to my heavenly Father: "Show me your way, Lord!" My father had been released early from custody in Burma and was now at last with us. I prayed with him for guidance for my life. I knew that he had always prayed that God would use me in his service, but he had never tried to talk me into it.

My mum didn't want to pray with me about this. I know that she actually implored God *not* to lead me to become a pastor. My father's way of life was so full of deprivation, in her view, that she wanted to spare her son from this or a similar fate. Although she had prayed at my birth for me to become a preacher of the gospel, her terrible experiences of persecution and deprivation had changed her. She didn't doubt God's love and had not abandoned her faith in him, but she didn't want her son to run headlong into this danger zone. She had confessed to me some time previously that she had actually prayed this as early on as my eighth birthday. My father was at that time in prison yet again, and the police had trashed our house. I can understand her feelings totally now – she is, after all, my mother.

26

What's to become of me?

So I went to see the Christians who had helped us out of China. Their leader greeted me cheerfully as usual and asked me how things were going.

"Not very well," I said.

"Yes, I've heard that you had to give up the technical college because your German wasn't good enough. So what do you want to do now?"

"I really don't know," I replied in desperation.

At this he invited me to go to a Bible school.

"But that's the whole problem! How can I do a course at a Bible school in Germany when I just can't get the language right?"

He put his arm round my shoulders and comforted me: "Isaac, this language thing is best learned among friends. In the Bible school you would have friends who could help you with the language, and you can just sit there in the lessons and listen without any pressure. You understand what you understand, and the rest will come bit by bit. You know the subject matter well already – and you'll see how quickly you'll be able to understand the biblical texts themselves."

This seemed a bit like clutching at straws, but the bit about gradually easing myself in seemed sensible to me. So two days later I packed my things and travelled with one of the brothers to the Beröa Theological College at Erzhausen near Darmstadt. I didn't know what kind of theological college I was entering from a spiritual point of view. Even a few months in Germany had shown me that the Christian community there was quite splintered. What sort of place was I going to? Was it charismatic? Evangelical? Community church? Baptist, or maybe even a denomination that I had not encountered yet? We simply went there and I had to trust that it was the correct path.

The director wanted me to give it a try. I could stay there for a year at no cost, mostly to learn German but also to register for theological subjects. Only as much as I could cope with: no pressure, no stressful need to achieve; only friends who understood me and would help me.

When I joined the class I was laughed at to start with. I stood there like a stupid boy. The others giggled about me and whispered to their neighbours. Today I would probably join in too, as I was wearing a Brazilian football shirt that was far too big for me. I was so proud of this shirt! In China no one had cared about the size of your shirt; the main thing was to have a striking shirt belonging to "your" team. Part of the problem was that, as a Chinese person, I am quite a lot smaller than young German people. With my short hair and long shirt I must have looked like a thirteen-year-old, although I was actually nineteen at the time.

I tried to save the situation and greeted the other students in my very Chinese German. The result of this was that they split their sides laughing. I wanted the ground to swallow me up, but the director came over to me and said: "We've never greeted a student this cheerfully before. You're most welcome here."

Now the students too became aware that their laughter had unsettled me greatly, so they came up to me one by one, greeted me with a handshake, told me their names, and spoke a few pleasantries, which I couldn't of course understand.

I soon started to get on well with the young people. We learned together, but we also had parties and played sports. They were amazed by what I had been through, observing: "Isaac, you have suffered so much for God and overcome so many disadvantages; we wouldn't have been able to do that." They even started coming to me to ask about spiritual matters, about confession and protection, and about suffering and staying true to God.

My relationships with my fellow students developed well, but the lessons proved to be a misery for me. As well as theology and German there were more languages to learn, namely Greek and Hebrew. It seemed more and more clear to me that if I couldn't get a grip on these, then the Lord would not be able to use me.

My uncertainty persisted: what should I do with my life? No way did I want to be a preacher. There were loads of talented people out there who could become preachers.

"Lord, find them from among your people," I said to him. "And if it has to be a Chinese person, well, Lord, there are 1.3 billion others – choose one of *them*. Yet I *do* want to do your will."

Then I met a Chinese Christian who had a top job with Deutsche Bank in Frankfurt.

He asked me: "Isaac, what do you *really* want to do? Don't you fancy going into banking? We Chinese are going to be the new world power, and we're going to need a lot of people with good principles and Christian values to take the lead in this. You speak German and Chinese, the main prerequisite for a great career."

Bank director – I could quite see myself in that role. I was better than average at maths, and pretty good at dealing with money. The idea took firm root in me as I took the light railway home.

On the way I had a good look at the business people in their smart suits, with their shiny black briefcases and gold watches. I could get used to the prospect of looking like that. I imagined myself sitting at a big desk in a banking firm, in suit and tie, with my own assistant and a laptop always at hand. The salary of a top bank manager would provide me with security. But I was so lost in these dreams that I passed my station and forgot to get off. Was that a sign from God that the banking business was overstepping the mark for me – or rather for *him*?

Naturally there were plenty of people urging me to accept the role of preacher. Passing foreign evangelists in particular seemed inspired by the idea of seeing the son of the "famous" Brother Yun in the pulpits of the world. But that was not my aim. I would rather have a decent job and ensure stability and security for myself and my future family. I liked the idea of having a few of life's luxuries, which I had been deprived of throughout my childhood.

The example of my father kept putting me off the thought of becoming a preacher. A life full of privation, being on the run, and being treated with hostility (which he was still experiencing even from so-called pious people in the West), and zero family life – I just didn't want that.

I was so unsure about my future at that moment that the brooding pursued me even into my dreams. The uncertainty sometimes troubled me so much that I wept in secret.

The syllabus at Beröa included practical training. I was assigned to go to Russia with a group of experienced Christians. We went to Moscow, to Omsk, to the superb Lake Baikal, and finally to Novosibirsk. I was greatly moved by it all. I saw countless people suffering from alcohol abuse: men, women, and even a horrifying number of young people. We saw drug addicts who looked so wild and neglected that I was actually afraid of them. But I also found that such people came to faith as a result of our gospel work and found freedom from their addictions. Ours were just simple words, only roughly translated, and yet they touched people's innermost hearts, and they threw their wretched, ruined lives aside in order to receive new life from Jesus.

The local Christians were clearly very concerned about involving young people in this situation, but we flew on to gain experience of other aspects of the work.

I was thousands of kilometres from Germany, but the gnawing question of my future had come with me on the trip. I had become confused again about whether God maybe did want me to take up the saving work of evangelization. But then I reflected on how much strength I had needed for this work, and that the strain of the journey had not been inconsiderable. So was it not for me after all?

Just as I had taken the problem to Russia, so now it travelled devotedly and doggedly back with me. Normal lessons continued in the Bible school, including worship each morning. I sat once again in the chapel, listened and had only one thought: what should I do? What was God's plan for me? Soon my year would be up – and then what?

I can't remember what the sermon was about that morning. It was a song that brought me salvation:

> Your grace is sufficient for me;
> Your strength is made perfect
> when I am weak.
> All that I cling to
> I lay at your feet.
> Your grace is sufficient for me.

> (Extract taken from the song "Your Grace is Sufficient" by Marty Nystrom, copyright © 1991 Integrity's Hosanna! Music/ Kingswaysongs.)

We sang this song with the band, and then the pianist urged us to sing it unaccompanied – each person as if for him- or herself.

Suddenly I knew: "This is it!" Tears came into my eyes and I couldn't go on singing. I sank to my knees and sobbed like a child.

"God, I have given my life to you so often before; I'm giving it to you again today, and my whole future with it. I say yes to your will; I *will* become a bearer of your good news."

The other Bible students were quite shocked, because I didn't usually react so emotionally to things. The director, who knew of my inner struggle, called over to me softly: "Congratulations, Isaac." I had finally passed the most important test of my life.

27

The "dusty country"

I was now finally, totally convinced that I should become a preacher. Not only had my father and many other Christians pointed constantly in this direction, but in the depths of my heart I had always known that this was my path. Yes, I had been afraid of it and had closed my ears and my heart to it, but now everything was so plain and so clear to me that I felt quite relieved and happy.

I stood up, wiped the now no longer sorrowful tears from my face, embraced my fellow students and called out confidently: "Brothers, I am going to preach the gospel, on land, at sea, and in the air, without reserve and with all my strength and all my time."

Applause crackled around the room as they shared my joy.

I had no further problems at college. I no longer learned mechanically but with a firm goal in mind. Whenever I had a moment free from studying, I planned my future service. I saw myself among young people as I walked through the pedestrian zone of a big city and spoke to the people there about God. I saw myself in pulpits and in hospitals, preaching and having discussions with Chinese students, of whom there are many in Germany.

But now came the big question of whether I could get a post. What would happen after Bible school?

At Beröa we had many visits from foreign Christians, missionaries, and short-term workers from all over the world. Naturally they would always ask us students where we wanted to serve. You could go anywhere from Beröa. A missionary who had known my family for a long time once visited us at the college. After the inevitable question as to what I would be doing, he laid his hand on my shoulder and said: "When you finish here, you should leave this dusty country."

This remark troubled me for some days. By "dusty country" he of course meant Germany. Should I go to Singapore, and perhaps get to know a Chinese girl and marry her? Or should I go to England or America, where the possibilities for missionary work were unlimited? Ought I to leave Germany? At first glance, much in the church here *did* seem dry and dusty. Countless congregations used a stale, rigid liturgy, and there was little living faith. People bickered over theological questions instead of developing strategies for mission and evangelism. Unfortunately this is true; I have seen it for myself.

But that is only half the truth. There are also many truly devout men and women in Germany, who are marvellous examples of gospel work and selfless love of their neighbour. It was, after all, the community of believers in Germany that had saved my father and our whole family.

I felt sorry for this "dusty country". I realized that I had learned to love Germany. No, I wanted to stay here.

I wanted to learn more from the Christians here and contribute to bringing the gospel to many more people in this country. But how?

After finishing college, all the Bible students had to do a practical placement. I was invited to give a trial sermon in Geislingen in Baden-Württemberg. At lunch the pastor asked me if I would like to do my training in Geislingen. To be honest, I wasn't sure. By Chinese standards a town of 26,000 inhabitants is a mere village, and my desire was to work in a city with pedestrianized zones and students. But it was what God wanted for me.

I stayed there for two and a half years, until I got my own congregation. But that is another story.

28

When I think of China …

Of course I think about my own country a lot. I hear of growing congregations. My friends send emails; they call me and report on all that God is doing in China. It still isn't possible for me to go back there. The names of my father and our family are almost certainly still on the lists of wanted criminals. But it will become possible again in God's good time.

I dream of being able to help the church in China with my international experience. I would like to be a bridge-builder between the German church, with its many spiritual experiences, and the Chinese church. A bridge-builder, too, between a country of almost unlimited freedom and one in which there is still persecution and tyranny. Our experiences of persecution and escape can help Germany to view Chinese Christians in a different light, and people might be able to recognize God's modern miracles. This might comfort Christians in Germany, who are saddened by church disputes and shrinking congregations.

When 10,000 come to faith in China, the angels in heaven rejoice over it. But they also rejoice when any individual man or woman in Germany accepts Jesus as Lord and begins to live for him.

I am well aware that in Germany there is a lot of prejudice towards China. Even the man on the street talks about the "Chinese threat", meaning Communism or the growing economic power of China.

Fear of people disappears when you get to know them. I advise everyone who can to go on a visit to China. Don't just let yourself be thrilled by our cultural highlights, but go into the churches, seek out the Christians, and experience what God is doing there. You will come back with renewed courage and new friends – and you don't need to be afraid of your friends.

***

If you would like to know more about the work of AVC – *Aktion für verfolgte Christen und Notleidende* / Action for Persecuted and Needy Christians – you will find information at the following address. You can also obtain copies of the bi-monthly free magazine *AVC-report*:

AVC
Hassiaweg 3
63667 Nidda
Germany
Tel. +49 (0)6043-4524
mail@avc-de.org
www.avc-de.org

The Heavenly Man

With Paul Hattaway

The Heavenly Man is the intensely dramatic story of how God took a young, half-starved boy from a poor village in Henan Province and used him mightily to preach the gospel despite horrific opposition.

Brother Yun is one of China's house church leaders, a man who despite his relative youth has suffered prolonged torture and imprisonment for his faith. Instead of focusing on the many miracles or experiences of suffering, however, Yun prefers to emphasize the character and beauty of Jesus.

This astonishing book will form a watershed in your spiritual life.

Brother Yun travels widely and speaks around the world from his current base in Germany. Paul Hattaway has written several books on the Chinese church and is the director of Asia Harvest.

ISBN 978-1-85424-597-7 £8.99 UK

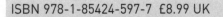
www.lionhudson.com/monarch

MONARCH